Fai

Faith - The Working Factors

Faith -The Working Factors

By Terry Leaman

Faith –The Working Factors
By T.M.Leaman
Copyright © 2024
All rights reserved

Faith - The Working Factors

Index

Foreword by the Author	Page	7
1 **You *Have* Faith**	Page	13
2 ARISE! Cross over the line!	Page	19
3 Put off the Old Faith ……	Page	27
4 The Safety Factor	Page	35
5 'I will fear no evil'	Page	44
6 Faith going public.	Page	53
7 The 'Rules' of faith.	Page	58
8 Putting Hope back ….	Page	75
9 The Holy Spirit – God's Factor	Page	82
10 Freedom and moving forward	Page	88
11 Doubt, - the disabling factor	Page	95
12 The Results of Faith	Page	103
13 Belief is the key.	Page	113
14 Partnering with God	Page	125
15 Reign – Faith ruling.	Page	133
16 The Surrender Factor	Page	141
17 The Sustenance Factor	Page	149
18 Faith Tested Out	Page	156
19 Faith - Not being seduced away	Page	167
22 Faith - the LIFE Factor	Page	184
23 Faith – Pleasing the Father	Page	192
24 What this book is all about	Page	201
25 Courage –Seeing what we have	Page	207
26 The Triune Factor	Page	214
27 The DOMINION of Faith	Page	223
28 GREATER is He that is in you	Page	230

Faith, Mighty Faith the problem sees and looks to God alone, it laughs at impossibilities and cries, "IT SHALL BE DONE!"

Charles Wesley

Foreword by the Author

Faith, to get it, or to get it and keep it working in your life, *seems* often to be an impossible task. Many believers appear to become either overwhelmed by trying to get faith and give up the fight because that's what it feels like, a fight, or else they don't seem to believe that real people can **actually have** a working faith. By working faith I really mean a faith that sees people sick for example and believes that they can pray for them in the Bible prescribed way and see them healed. Or to look at another example of working faith, to see a real obstacle in life and pray it out of existence. Take Jonah as a specimen example, he is in the belly of the whale and in that dire position it says that he prayed *in* his prayer. In other words, he found a new way to pray in a crisis that he had never done before. Whatever he *did* pray that day worked and he got a good response, the right response. This was a great prayer!

There are many issues that we are unaware of when dealing in faith matters and this is for many reasons. Sometimes we are blind to all the factors of why our faith doesn't work and sometimes we

Faith - The Working Factors

are just simply blind to the fact that we *all do actually* have faith. Often, too, we need proof that we *do* have faith. The best clue is to read what God says and find the scripture that tells us, 'To each is given *the* measure of faith'. And then there are those who know or at least have an inkling, a suspicion that they have some faith but don't know that their faith can actually perform a miracle when set in motion. And then again, there are those who know that faith can do miracles but fall short when thinking that *their* faith is given to them by God, who can do the impossible. We will discuss this later but Jesus in the boat on the lake in the middle of a storm with the disciples, stills the storm by speaking to the storm with His faith but then turns to them and asks in effect, 'Why did *you* not still the storm?'

Until we are challenged with the reality of who we are and what we can do, faith sits dormant. The sad thing about this is that so many people lose out in life with friends and relatives who are sick etc and ***could have been*** healed or helped by faith.

Faith - The Working Factors

Faith is for using. It is not a nice looking title on the bookshelf. The contents of the book of faith are both stimulating and exciting to read.

I pray that when you read the rest of this book that God's Spirit, the author of faith, will inspire you and activate something in you that you didn't know you had the sheer volume of and that His great faith will just come alive in you. He put it there for a reason, to help all your 'situations' so that when times are testing, you will ride out the storm easily. In church one day during the Covid epidemic I was speaking with a couple about how they were faring, I remarked that we had not had Covid at all and the brother said to me, 'Oh we've both had it ***but we sailed right through it***'. Now for me that also expresses faith and its power.

So read with faith. Hear with faith. I often say to people, pick up the Bible and as you read, look for the faith in the words and *see* just what they will do.

Can I also say; please read this book with careful deliberation. So many read quickly and fly over the pages, not really considering that the stories

Faith - The Working Factors

came from an actual event where faith demonstrated its power. I try to quote either directly from my own experience or get others to dictate their own accounts of their faith working. This is so important in portraying truthfully the things that have happened because trust is vital where faith is concerned as you will see.

I pray that God will speak to your heart, to the core of you as you read this book. For me it is pointless to even read such a book if we are not going to glean life changing truths from it. God wants to help us in every situation in life**; He gave us faith for that reason.**

TO GOD WHO MAKES MY FAITH WORK RIGHT

FAITH – The working Factors

CHAPTER ONE
You Have *Faith!*

Most people seem to understand faith to be something that only special people have. So let's take a look at something very fundamental about the human race. To set the scene to what I have to tell you, we need to do some simple thinking that many people overlook. Firstly, we were created by God in the beginning, so read the Genesis 1 account of our origin.

When He created us, the Almighty made a statement before He began His work. He said, "Let us make man in our image and in our likeness". Note that He uses two descriptions to form the process, 'Image' and 'likeness'. We get the word imagination from the word image, it's a mental, mind shape that we get when we 'see' something with our thoughts. It's a mind concept of something. In this case, God is imagining or to be more precise, 'Imaging' what He is going to create. He wants to create another like Himself **with** His own concept and **in** His own concept. So

Faith - The Working Factors

out of His knowledge of Himself He 'images' His creation to be. He also has imaged the *physical* form of Himself, His *likeness*, His physical self. With the initial creation, He also breathes breath - *His Spirit*, into that creation and man becomes a living soul. Adam, the outcome of His imagination, comes into being made in God's Image, Likeness and has a Spirit life just like God, Triune.

God did not leave anything out when He created Adam, that's not God's way. He gave him arms legs, torso, brain…. All that He has Himself. Why have I started this book this way? Because I want to point out that when He made us, God left nothing out, which means He also gave us one of His great assets, **Faith**. We got a free will too because God has a free will. God is unfettered in His thinking because He cannot be overpowered, forced or coerced to do anything against His will, He is known in fact as 'The Almighty'. So did Adam and Eve have this attribute in the beginning? Yes. They were unfettered in their power, they had dominion over everything in the earth, just like God. It was satan who suggested that there were things they didn't have but in fact God gave them

Faith - The Working Factors

everything of Himself. It was only after sinning, rebelling against God that they became limited in power and strength. In rebelling against God they resisted having all His attributes and lessened themselves.

So the really important thing I want us to understand is that we got faith from God, like we got everything else. In fact in the new testament of the Bible we read in the original King James version, "We have the faith of Christ". Not faith *in* Christ, we put our faith (our trust) in Him but we have the faith **OF** Christ. It appears at least 6 times that way.

The point we need to understand at the beginning of this book is that we **HAVE** faith.

When one day I addressed a group of young men talking about faith and telling of some of the things God had done in my life by faith, one young man said, "It's ok for you but I don't have *your* faith". My reply was, 'Yes you do, more than that, you have God's faith'. The scripture says clearly, 'We have all been given *the* measure of Faith'." Romans 12:3. You see it's not what we feel that

Faith - The Working Factors

counts, it's the facts that count and *the* fact, as given to us by God is that we all have the measure of faith. Like arms, legs and all our other limbs and faculties, we have been given faith too. We have a normal length arm or leg. We have a normal amount of faith too. The argument from the young man was then, 'Well mine doesn't work like yours does', he replied. Now that may be true but it didn't mean that his faith couldn't work if given the right stimulus.

I am fortunate enough to have seen many miracles at various times, apart from hearing faith accounts either from the Bible or from people, so my faith had received a kick start as it were when quite young.

Most people, we often say, are turned from being a non-believer to a believer as soon as they see a miracle. Others become believers when they hear a report of a miracle and believe it. Either way, their faith gets kick started.

The major point I'm making here is that working faith is available for all and is already here **in** us.

Faith - The Working Factors

What is needed is to make it operate the correct way?

Before we are 'born again' often there is no basis for faith to work much. We may have a basic trust that God can do many things if we understand who He is and what He can do but until we have contact again with His Spirit, it is merely a dead idea. Once the life of God's Spirit enlivens our soul again and regenerates us, that is a different matter. Our character, our 'image', given to us as when Adam was created, is reconstituted when we are born again and rebuilt to God's specification again, alive and active once more. We need to consider the term, 'Born Again' in more detail perhaps for the matter to sink in to our conscious beings again, for that's what we are, we are re-birthed, we have a brand new start.

So for a start to this subject, I hope the picture is clearer, even if you have some faith active already. God has made it possible for us all to work in faith and be active to believe for all sorts of things to be able to happen. Things that are normally outside the realms of possibility and things that may be far-fetched or difficult to imagine because of the

Faith - The Working Factors

ways we have been brought up, I hope will become possible, with God's sight, *active* once again in us.

God never meant for us to be blind sighted with regard to ways out of our various predicaments, He *always* wanted us to see our way out of troubles. He has never left us helpless, satan left us that way but God ALWAYS made a way of escape out of trouble, in every sense of the word. I remember God speaking to us in a house meeting through a prophet one day, He said, *'Whenever you are in trouble and there seems to be no way out, look for the way of escape, for I have provided one'.* Now THAT is the basis of Faith. Look at this statement God makes, it's well backed up by various scriptures throughout the Bible but this is a standard method by which God invigorates and revitalises our faith, bringing it to life and making it active. He speaks to us.

Like our arms and legs, we have a body/mind member that is called faith. We use it even when we are not born again, it's just that without God's inspiration firing it up, it gets used for many other less useful or bad things.

Faith - The Working Factors

Instead of using it for good, we 'believe' we will fail or be left *without* an escape route from trouble.

All of our faculties and abilities, because of rebellion entering our race, can be used in one of two ways, either for right or for wrong. To put this in a more Biblical way, we live ***right*eously** or ***unright*eously**. If I have a limb, say my arm, I can either do good with my arm and assist people or I can fight with it, punching and hurting people.

So it is with everything I have, whether with my possessions, I can give and be generous or be mean and withhold my possessions from others, hoarding and not helping them when they need help.

So we've laid a basic foundation for our relationship to God, we either agree with His ways or we don't. When we agree with His ways, we get His backing and assistance, when we don't, we stand on our own and often struggle or worse in life.

Chapter TWO
ARISE! Cross over the line!

In Joshua chapter 1, God says to Joshua, "***Arise, go over this Jordan***, you and all this people, ***to the land which I have given them***".

Promised land. God has promised us so much but we have to cross over the obstacles to get it. That's not difficult, we just need to accept what God says and use our faith. The secret is to believe what God says and 'go for it'. Take a moment and just think. God will never lie to you. If He says a thing, He fully means it. If He says, 'I am the Lord that heals you', then your response with faith should be, 'You are the Lord that heals me'.

Promised land is *our* land that God, who doesn't lie, has set aside for *us* to inhabit. **It's already ours**. Look in Matthew 6 for example at 'the Lord's Prayer'. Jesus says, "**Pray this,** - 'Our Father who is in Heaven….. Give us this day *our* daily bread". It's already YOUR daily bread, it doesn't have God's name on it, Jesus says it's already **your *daily bread*.**

Faith - The Working Factors

'Promised land' is already earmarked and given, you just have to take hold of it. The way you do it is by using your faith.

SO let's go back to Joshua chapter one again. God says, ARISE. This is how faith goes into action. Get yourself up and RISE. Lift yourself up in your faith above your bad situation or 'lack' situation and ***RISE***. Faith is all about rising up. Consciously determine to do what God has told you to do in a situation and *rise up* above it. What He *says* has a rising ability built into it. You see, the character of God is a rising-up character. His ways are naturally, to Him, rising-up ways, bettering ways, resurrecting ways. When He made us, He gave us His own character of being able to rise, it's called 'FAITH'. When we became born again, when we asked Him to forgive us and to come and live by His Spirit inside us, we were born once more but this time born of an incorruptible nature, a nature that has **rise** within it, i.e., **Faith.** *'That new nature has no fear or weakness. If it has any weakness then it is because we are limiting our faith or not giving it permission to operate'. We are talking of our old habits.*

Faith - The Working Factors

Faith doesn't take us down, it's dead religion and fear that does that. The gospel of Jesus, the *good news*, is that we now have the ability to get up above all our old life and problems. It's in our born again nature to do that. We just need to recognise it and see that it's now *in us* to rise.

WE HAVE FAITH. I don't think we see it very clearly, that we now have, since we got born again, a new living being inside of us. I always remember one day studying the word of God and it became alive. I got a real kick from what God was telling me and became elated and joyful at what God had said, almost dancing around my room. But in the moments that followed, satan began to pick at my new revelation and tried to take it from me. Then all of a sudden a voice spoke up inside me and said, "You're too late satan, I've swallowed it". I sat there mesmerised. Who's voice was that?, I asked myself. Then as I analysed the phrase, I realised that it was my new born again being talking and it was telling satan to get his hands off my stuff. "God gave me this revelation, this is mine, get your hands off it!" I returned to the joy again and enjoyed what God had spoken to my soul. I had not realised just how

Faith - The Working Factors

alive my spirit and soul was. I was a new born again being and my soul was shouting about it and what's more was exercising its right to tell satan where to get off.

Faith does that. *It rises up and takes dominion over problems*, whether the problems are sickness, bad attitudes, wrongs, lying behaviour, lack of funds, weakness, pain or whatever is trying to pull you down, faith pulls you back up into the heavenly realm where your sprit now rightfully resides.

One year, I was about to depart for Uganda on a mission to preach the gospel, I would fly in three days time. Laying in bed on my own that morning, with my wife visiting our daughter and her family in the USA, I mused on what would happen during the mission. I pondered on where we might go and what churches we would visit maybe and so on. As I contemplated, there seemed to be a dark cloud over one area of the mission, I rather felt that I was short of finances maybe. Instantly God took my mind to Genesis 1 when 'the earth was shapeless and empty', my finances had that sort of feeling to them. It said, 'Darkness was on the face of the

Faith - The Working Factors

mission'. I could, in my mind's eye, see darkness over my finances for the trip. Then my mind skipped to what God did. He spoke! He said, *"Let there be light!"* I saw it immediately, 'I must speak light over my finances'. I lifted my arms above the blankets and spoke loudly, "Let there be light!" My soul just became alive and I felt the life of those words lifting my spirit. It took my imagination by storm and I began speaking light over all sorts of problem areas in my life. I spoke light over my family, that God would save them, I spoke over many situations that needed God's blessing and I had a great time lying there in bed with my arms outstretched over problem areas, using my newly found *vision*.

After breakfast I went to the bank and drew out all the money Helen and I had put away for the mission and sent it to Uganda ready for my arrival there in 4 days time. As I left the Western Union office and crossed the road, my phone rang. *"Hello Terry, this is Ruth* (a lady from our midlands fellowship). *I've just been telling the Lord that I must send Terry some funds for his missions".* She didn't know that I was soon to leave for Uganda. "Anyway, I'm sending you a cheque immediately in the post by first class mail to help with your missions!" I was amazed. I think the vernacular term is 'Gobsmacked'. Next day the letter arrived with the cheque…., for £1,000!

You see where this is going? This is where we *belong*. **Our *promised land*** is our faith land where we believe that God will provide all that we need. We have to ARISE to take it but the realisation that it is ours by right is what we have to appreciate. We have to cross over the hurdles and obstructions and walk step by step and claim the territory. God said to Joshua, "Every place that the sole of your feet treads on, I have ***given you!***" ***So you determinedly, step there***, press your feet firmly onto the ground and claim it. Say what God says to say over dark situations, "Let there be light!" Drive out the darkness of the circumstances and let your faith speak light.

"THIS IS MINE in Almighty God's name". But you have to let you spirit *arise*. It has to be claimed by your faith.

Faith - The Working Factors

God repeatedly speaks to our souls once we begin to claim our territory. He keeps saying, "ARISE". It's our new nature to use our faith and get up out of our mess and enter our Heaven realm. We have a Kingdom, we are meant to rule and reign as believers and put down the wrong and the evil. Jesus came to this world to 'destroy the works of the devil'. The Holy Spirit is here now to do the same, He is inside us here, to destroy satan's works.

In the *promised* land, as Joshua and Caleb saw, were giants. Does God lead them across Jordan to trap them in a land inhabited by giants that will destroy them? No. In the *promised* land they will have power over all the giants, however big they are, simply because God has told them to ARISE. This 'RISING' power in them is able to do the impossible. Jesus said, "With God all things ARE possible" but *then* He says, "If *you* believe all things **ARE** possible. The reason why I've highlighted the word 'ARE' is because recently God changed the emphasis on the phrase to me, to make me see that it's a fact. God really makes it possible.

Faith - The Working Factors

But we have to **decide** to ARISE. God will not overrule our free will. Unless we give our will into His hands and let go of the old ideas and thinking, we will hardly change. We still retain our 'free' will but now it's more free because it's now employed by our faith. Of course if we have a leaning towards Him, He sees it and tries to help us within the context of our wishes but to get the full benefit of God's help we need to say clearly to Him, "I *want* to change, I *want* to do what is right. *I want* a real working Faith that does *all* that you designed for it to do. Use me Father and take the doubt and fear away". Decisiveness is what God needs to see, a definite, clear abandon of our old ways and a new path over the obstacles and doubts adopted. I always say to people when ministering, "Give as much of yourself to the Almighty as you can see to give Him at any time. When a new aspect of surrendering to Him comes to your mind, don't hesitate, give that area over to Him". Arise, stop the rot, lift up your head and attitude to God and start winning things. Use your Faith.

Faith - The Working Factors

CHAPTER 3
Put off the Old Faith, Put on the new Faith

Ephesians 4 says for us to 'put off the 'old man (or woman) and His/her ways and put on the new man (or woman) renewed in the spirit of your mind'.

If our faith isn't making it, if we aren't seeing supernatural answers to our problems, we need to have a working faith. Hebrews 11 says that Faith is the substance of the things we hoped for. 'Hope<u>d</u>' means that it's not here yet but we've put ourselves forward for it and aligned ourselves with the idea of getting what God has said we can have. Hope for healing is a good example of this.

If I have a sickness or disease, I *hope* that God will heal me of it. I express to Him that I want Him to heal me. I ask Him. ***Then*** I can make that request more powerfully to Him by quoting to Him *what He said* on the matter. **He** says, "I am the Lord that heals you", so **I** say that to Him in the form of *my* response, ***"You are the Lord that heals me!"*** What I've done is to take up His promise and showed that I understand what He said on the matter of healing. I'm putting myself in the frame

27

Faith - The Working Factors

for what He promised me and shown direct meaning on the matter. I've personalised the matter. I have asked for definite help from Him in the matter of healing my sickness.

Defining what we mean is important. We state that we understand what He said about us being healed, it also removes any ambiguity, any doubt in *our* minds about what God said we could have, if we asked for it. ***That's important.*** We do need to show ourselves, our conscious minds, that we have an understanding of His promises and have acted rightly about it, that we have demanded our rightful requirements from Him and we know that we should get them. After all, He promised them if we asked Him. Jesus said that if we asked the Father for anything in His, ***Jesus'*** name, we would get it.

The doubts will arise of course. So let's look at this in the context of Ephesians 4. 'Put off the old faith that doesn't work because doubts are clogging up our thinking'. Let's now clear our minds and renew them with what God said about faith. - **"If you believe, nothing wavering, but believe in your heart, in the core of you** (I'm

28

Faith - The Working Factors

paraphrasing this and putting together several legitimate statements about it) **that God has already promised you this, then you will have what you are believing for.**" Call that, the 'Terry Leaman amplified version'. But see now, this is what we *should* be doing, accepting the *whole* word of God on the matter and letting our faith put together all the things God has legitimately said we can have and grasp them with our hope and belief ready for our faith to use them.

In the Lord's prayer (Matthew 6), Jesus says what we should pray and most importantly HOW we should pray. Watch what He says…, ***"In this manner pray"***. He shows us the *attitude* that we should pray with. Notice there is no 'please' or 'thank you' in the Lord's prayer. Jesus means us to get serious when asking our heavenly Father for something. He is not saying that we should be arrogant or disrespectful in any way, He's merely telling us to accept who we are and state it in honesty. He's promised it, so put away your doubts and be firm in asking Him. (There are demons and angels and fallen angels and all manner of spiritual forces listening to your prayer). So begin praying as Jesus said to begin. ***"OUR***

Faith - The Working Factors

FATHER". This is **who** is praying, a real, true, child of God, so *identify yourself* as that and speak boldly to your Heavenly Father asking for what it is that you want. You have rights that He gave you and those rights affect your faith when you acknowledge those rights. ***Then*** be even more specific as Jesus also said to do, "Our Father, WHO IS IN HEAVEN". You are not a child of satan any more, you are not a 'child of hell'. You are a son or daughter of the Almighty God. So declare it boldly before all the doubters and those who would deny who you are. SAY IT with right attitude, *personalise* it. "**MY FATHER** WHO IS IN HEAVEN." Then call to book all who do not respect His name, (My Father) HALLOWED BE YOUR NAME!" Holy and respected BE your name. In other words, whoever is disrespecting God's name, ***call time on their disrespect***. Father in Heaven, **Hallowed** BE *your* name!

The Lord's prayer, (**our** prayer now because He gave it to ***us*** to speak) is a set of statements, not requests but ***respectful demands***. These are dominion words.

Faith - The Working Factors

Remember that Adam and Eve were given dominion over everything in the earth. From God's perspective, that should have remained, they should have always had dominion but rebellion (sin) against God took it off them. Remember that everything sin took from us is recovered in salvation.

Listen to something Oral Roberts once said at a Pre-Crusade Pastors seminar,
"Jesus Christ has come to take off you what satan put on you,
He came to take out of you what satan put in you,
He came to put on you what satan took off you.
And put in you what satan took out.
He has come to redeem you!"

Part of our recovery is our use of our dominion. Examine closely the attitude of the prayer as Jesus stated it. Look at all the **command** words…. "Thy Kingdom **COME!**" "Thy will **BE** done!"….. "**On earth** AS IT IS IN HEAVEN!" This is powerful and *God is giving you the words to say that will bring it about*. "**GIVE US THIS DAY** our daily bread". The bread, Jesus is saying, is already yours, it's OUR daily bread. Also,

31

Faith - The Working Factors

demand your forgiveness, **"Forgive us"**. God has already forgiven you, so fiercely expect to be forgiven, God is serious about you being forgiven. In the middle of all His pain on the cross, *the one thing that matters to Jesus is that you are forgiven.* He says, "Father forgive them!"

The words of God are *so* important to our faith. They are the backbone of what we believe we can have. We need to understand legitimately what is available to us to ask for. *If we are not sure of what we can have, we will not ask for it.* We must though, see what else Jesus is saying when we ask for forgiveness, we must also forgive or we don't get to be forgiven. Jesus in Matthew 6 is very clear about it. God demands us to be just and fair, if we are to be forgiven, then *we* must forgive.

Putting off the old and putting on the new is the pattern of things that is good and right to adopt.

Remember that we have 'been 'transferred' from the kingdom of darkness, the place of deception and fraud and lies, to the Kingdom of God's dear Son'. All that Jesus did, He said that *we* could do and greater things even. But it takes us to RISE

Faith - The Working Factors

and act with the faith that God gave us to use. He also gave us His nature, the nature of Almighty God.

Putting off the old man is as much a need as putting on the new man. In fact, <u>we can't keep the old man and as well have the new man.</u> The way we get the new man/woman is to put off our old nature and his/her ways, in other words, 'stop doing the old stuff'. Ask for forgiveness and start living the new way. New faith is the new way. We have been using old faith. Yes, our faith has never gone missing, it has just been used for other things.

We 'believed' we could only fail, we believed the lies of satan, we lived with depression and failure, failing to see what God had all along laid up for us, we believed all those sorts of things were our life. 'But God, who is rich in mercy because of His great love wherewith He loved us, even when we were dead in our trespasses and sins, ***made us alive together with Christ and raised us up together with Him".***

Faith - The Working Factors

See there it is again. "Has *raised* us up together with Him". He raises us. He tells us to get our ways right, *'ARISE'*. Don't stay in lack or in deficit in the bank of life, be fruitful. Now that's God's way - Fruitfulness. Never beaten, never in lack, never without a way of escape, **safe**. The God who gives you safety is your shepherd.

The transition from the old ways to the new is so important. Putting off the old Terry Leaman is a major action (believe me). Putting on the new Terry Leaman and coming under better management is safer and happier with faith doing its job well. Faith can do just that, it can transition you from one bad route in life to a good, profitable and safe path through life. SO **ARISE!** Transition, put off the old and put on the new.

Chapter four
The Safety Factor

Many don't consider the 'safety factor' of faith. But you can read in the Bible, of God being our refuge and strength, of him being a safe place in the time of storm. A factor of the Faith route is that we are safe with God's tools. We use them when we are under threat and 'under siege' by evil forces. Even destruction itself is destroyed by God's good power and God is always protective of His children, it's His good nature to be so. The nature of faith is to secure safety for us and to provide what we need, even what we desire. ***To be vulnerable is not within the terms of faith,*** far from it. Faith is an overcoming power in our new personality, put there to destroy what tries to destroy us.

Examine for a moment the things Jesus says we should do with our faith, "Cleanse the lepers, raise the dead, cast out demons". These are all decent and good things for the recipients of faith's actions. Lepers are healed, dead people are raised up and given life again and bad spirits are sent out of people to allow them peace again.

Faith - The Working Factors

'Faith works by Love' is a scripture that shows the nature behind faith, so faith is evidently a part of our new nature. Now who didn't feel safe in a loving environment?

So it's important to put off the old nature, the old man/woman and their ways and put on the new born again attitudes. It's right for us to feel safe again and feel part of the 'Good Shepherd's' flock. There is great safety in this.

Part of our being practising believers should be to upscale our faith and wilfully make it an act of power when needed. Part of this is to realise that our faith has not always acted when it should have, so *that* inaction needs to be put off as part of putting off the old faith. When we act *as* we should, *when* we should, we often create a safe haven for ourselves and our families and friends. There is great safety when we realise that God can heal us and do the things we need done.

The people of God throughout the Bible proved the safety factor of faith when believing God for their needs. Especially when moving against enemies they saw God deliver them and heal them and feed them and provide riches above their needs. God's way is a safe way and it is all part of the Faith route for our lives.

We don't have to go the hard route and the dangerous route. God has provided a safe route for us. Faith is given to us to make our lives easier, to destroy the hurdles and obstacles with. My wife has so often said that as she was driving through town in the car, she needed a parking place. As she drove near where she needed to park, almost always a car would pull out and leave an empty place and she would testify of God's amazing provision for her 'little' needs. But I've also seen God provide for her 'Big' needs. Now think about it for a moment, finding the right parking place can be a safer option especially when crossing major roads are concerned.

Life with God is more 'safe' than we realise.

Look at the statement that God gives us in Psalm 91… "I will give my angels charge over you ***to keep you*** in all your ways". Now that's comprehensive. ALL your ways!

Faith - The Working Factors

I well remember a period when I suffered a stroke. It was a Sunday morning and I got out of bed to shower before going to church. I took my shower and as I later stood at the sink in the bathroom, part of my lip went numb. I rubbed it a bit and thought, "That's odd". It recovered quickly but a few minutes later, it happened again and again after the same treatment. I continued to get ready for church.

As I walked into church that morning a brother said to me, "Are you ok? I replied that I felt a bit 'under the weather'. He asked if I would like him to pray for me. I said 'Yes, please do.' We stood in the aisle and he prayed for me as people flocked into the church. As we went to communion that morning and stood in the queue, I came over feeling very odd, shaky and light headed. As I took communion that morning, I took the bread and wine and claimed forgiveness and healing as part of God's covenant with us. As we drove home from Church in the car my eyesight began to give me some slightly odd pictures. As I went through the day, things seemed to get better, until I went to bed. As I climbed into bed that night my left arm went numb and then my left leg went

Faith - The Working Factors

numb too all the way down to my big toe. I reached over to the bedside cabinet and gave my wife a small file of olive oil that we kept for anointing the sick and told her to pray. Within around 5 minutes both my arm and leg returned to normal, my feeling was restored and all seemed well. We agreed that I would call the doctor in the morning.

On calling the surgery, the doctor said, "Come down immediately". On arrival at the surgery he gave me pills and sent me straightway to the ER at the local hospital. They fast tracked me and gave me a CT scan and many tests which revealed I had suffered a stroke. 'A bleed in the brain above the visual cortex', was the official verdict.

I was due to fly to Uganda on a mission in 3 days but was told I must not fly. During the following days my vision played up and I saw many odd things such as the things on the television ending up on the settee. Mmmm, yes, odd things.

But during that disturbing time, God spoke to me from Psalm 91 over and over again for around 5 days. "I will give my angels charge over you to keep you in all your ways!" He did too. I never suffered any recurrence of those symptoms. Some years later I had what they thought was a similar episode but they found nothing with MRI scans and all sorts of blood tests etc. The symptoms never returned. God kept His word. What was unusual too was that in the week after that post stroke period, I often had the feeling that there was someone in the room with me over to my left in the corner but every time I would look there was no one to be seen. But often in the corner of my eye, in my peripheral vision, there was movement, someone sitting and occasionally their arms would move and God would repeat again to my Spirit, "I have given my angels charge over you to keep you in all your ways".

Faith needs a catalyst, a spur to promote it and make it live. It's God's word that does that. If God says it, you can build your life on what He says. More to the point for this book, you build your faith on it.

A safe life is what everyone wants but they rarely turn to God in every way to claim their 'safe' world.

Faith - The Working Factors

Unless you *know* that your safety can come from God, you will not consider using your faith for it. But Faith is not just safety, *it is offensive* (in the good sense of the word) *in fighting off the enemies of our safety.* The fact that God in Psalm 91 says that He will give His angels charge over us in all our ways means that He wants us safe. Of course if we don't believe, then we don't come under His safety. But once 'Born again', we give ourselves into His hands and enter His 'safe zone'.

In Psalm 23 David speaks of walking through the valley of the shadow of death and fearing no evil. Now that's safety. A shepherd keeps a rod and staff and David says, 'Your rod and staff they comfort me'. The shepherd protects us with the rod and the staff extends out and reaches for us, to pull us to safety when we are in a precarious position. Either way we are protected by our shepherd.

Faith is here. Faith doesn't leave us when we are in danger. One of the fruits of God's Spirit is Faith. The Holy Spirit who is in us is always resident, with *Faith to keep us safe from predatory powers.*

41

Faith - The Working Factors

In the book of Ephesians we read of the 'Shield of Faith', so once again we have faith as that available protector. But what we need to do is to deploy it. Put it up, raise it up in front of you to prevent the enemy's offensive actions from reaching you. <u>What we are really doing is saying a big 'NO' to the enemy…. 'You have no access to me,… I'm out of bounds to you.</u> My territory is not available to you, I'm governed by the laws of God, namely, in this case, the laws of belief and faith'.

Faith is actually a law and in this matter, satan is against the law but more importantly the law is against satan and evil of all kinds. There is a better way to look at the subject too, in Romans 8:2 we read that, ***'The law of the Spirit of life in Christ Jesus has made us free (safe) from the law of sin and death'.*** Now that's another slant on things but note once again, our safety. We are made safe from the law of sin and death by the laws of God. Again the harmful things of the world are held at bay by the good laws of God.

Faith - The Working Factors

There are so many things that we are **saved** from — *safe from,* once we begin to agree with God's principles.

The one thing that the world has not understood is that if they want safety, then the only real route to it is with faith and trust in an Almighty God.

Chapter Five
'I will fear no evil'

What do you have? Fear or Faith? We can't possess both at the same time, not in the same area of our lives.

Let me illustrate. My wife was never apparently afraid of anything, a stronger person you would never meet, she would take anyone on, she had a clear will of her own and was fearless...... except when it came to flying. She would get on a plane and sit there gripping the seat arms, wanting to be left alone and her white knuckles said it all. It curtailed us from thinking of going anywhere by plane. So a brother and myself prayed for her and the fear and the fear left her.

That year I had extra pay from taking a lecturing post in Milton Keynes near London so we decided to take the children to Malta for a holiday in the sun. We boarded the plane at Cardiff airport and Helen sat with my son Matthew and I sat a few seats away with my two daughters, Abigail and Charlotte. The plane moved to the runway and waited in take-off position.

Faith - The Working Factors

Knowing my wife's previous indisposition to flying, my son looked nervously at his mother. "Matthew, this plane is going to go like a bat out of hell down the runway in a moment", she said a little nervously. The plane took off and levelled out a few minutes later, to which my wife excitedly said to us, "Look, my hands are warm and dry, they're not sweating, my head is dry too", she said, feeling her forehead. ***The fear had gone!*** **God had done His work well**. Of course He had, He doesn't work any other way.

We had a lovely holiday in Malta, made all the better for knowing that we didn't have to face the ordeal of seeing my wife racked by fear of flying.

While we were in Malta, a terrible plane crash occurred in Scotland UK. A terrorist bomb was detonated on board a Panam 747 aircraft above Lockerbie in Scotland. The plane crashed into the village killing many, many people and all those on board.

As I went to pick up the British newspapers from the newsagents that morning, my eyes met the scenes on the front covers of all the newspapers. I

Faith - The Working Factors

picked up our papers and all over the front pages in vivid colour, were graphic scenes of a huge airliner-shaped hole in the ground where a village once was. The devastation was everywhere.

Arriving back at the villa, Helen was sat on the balcony in the sun. I put the newspapers on the table facing her with the probing words, "So what do you think of that then?", and watched her reaction. She did a double-take as her eyes met the scenes. Then after a pause, I saw her spirit recover her composure and she said calmly, "I'm fine, the fear is gone!" And it was too, quite clearly GONE.

After the holiday we sat in the plane on the runway once more at Malta's Luqa Airport. My son was again sat by his mother and I was sat with the girls. As we sat there waiting for take-off, my son turned to Helen and asked, "Are you OK Mum?" Her answer was profound. She replied, "Matthew, this is the safest plane in the sky tonight, do you know why? It's because **I'm on it**". We have flown all over the world since.

We can either have faith or fear but not both. Faith is the antidote to fear, it will drive fear out when

Faith - The Working Factors

you live through the fear experience using your faith. Faith puts down fear when it is raised against it.

God's prophet in scripture says, "When the enemy comes in, like a flood the Spirit of the Lord will raise up a standard against him! "Isaiah 59:19. **And it's so true when you realise** *that inside us is a Spirit that raised Jesus from the dead.* What a standard, to think that our biggest ever problem, 'death', can be overturned by God's Spirit of life.

The Bible states that fear of death is responsible for us being in bondage all of our lives. Fear masquerades as all sorts of things from fear of dentists to fear of spiders, to fear of flying but what is behind all fear, ultimately is fear of death.

To deny satan any more ways to make us fear, Jesus took on death itself and conquered it, giving us power over it. Fear should not be a problem to us any more once we realise that we have been given power over it. Do you remember as a child maybe that you encountered a large dog and clung to your Father's leg, hiding yourself away from the dog. Do you remember the safety

Faith - The Working Factors

you felt and do you remember the fear taking a back seat? Or maybe your parent held your hand as you encountered something frightening in some other way? Well you used faith just then, you put your life into someone else's hands and rode out the storm. That's a good picture of faith right there. We take the words of God and put our trust in them and hide within them until the storm passes, knowing we can trust what He says.

'God *IS* our refuge and strength'. We derive power to live in times when danger is around. We deny the fear and use God's armour, the *shield* of faith.

Putting a hold on fear is the best thing we can do. I remember the awful fear that I had of dentists. I had suffered at the hands of poor dentists as a child and had some bad experiences. The fears lasted away into adulthood and was even irrational at times. When confronted with going to the dentist again, my stomach would turn over at the thought. It would make me want to run away from the surgery and I wanted to take flight rather than confront the dentist's drill or the gas he would give me to extract a tooth. Some would say this is

Faith - The Working Factors

rational fear but it was real torment of soul to me. There simply was no faith in the process that would endear me to know I was safe in those places.

I well remember God speaking to me one day in the dentist's chair at the dental hospital in Cardiff. I had a tooth up in the gums that they said might have to be extracted. The dentist had left the room saying, "I won't be long, I'll just check the X-ray pictures". As I waited in the quiet of the room, my heart pounded and my stomach just turned over at the thought of what was maybe coming. The feeling of dread was awful. But as I sat there, the voice of God spoke up in my soul, ***"You can do this with or without fear!"*** How could I do this without fear? It seemed a ridiculous idea and I questioned God over it. And then He spoke again. **"You can do this *with* or *without fear!*"** <u>God was serious</u>, of course He was. He always could be trusted in everything He said.

The dental surgeon returned to the room saying, "I think we will leave the tooth there for now" and a huge feeling of relief went on inside me.

Faith - The Working Factors

Some years later in a similar situation, I was at home taking a shower preparing for an operation in hospital, on my bowel. The same old feeling came back and that stomach churning fear haunted me again as I considered the day ahead of me. As I took my shower, Helen came into the bathroom and said, "I'll delay going to school for an hour and drive you to the hospital!" but as she did, something of faith rose inside me and it spoke up. "**No.** *I* am taking *me* to the hospital". My faith was providing the motivation to get me to the surgeon and it made the fear take a back seat. *I* was going to do it and my faith was rising up and taking the situation on.

Then all of a sudden I felt the stomach churning sensation rise up and up and up inside me until it made me retch and heave many times. I almost physically vomited as the fear rose up inside and left me. ***Then it was gone.*** The fear that haunted me all those years had GONE. Faith disposed of it and sent it packing. It's true, God's Spirit *is* more powerful than all of satan's power. I proved it that day, our Faith that God put within us at salvation is greater than all of the fears and dread that sin put in us.

Faith - The Working Factors

After that my soul became much calmed and restful in the similar situations that ensued in the coming years and my faith began to rise to newer heights.

I can tell you of similar occasions where I challenged different fears that I had and saw them leave, like the fear of public speaking for instance.
In taking on the fear to perform a singing engagement at a school concert, my faith stood up to be counted and told satan to get his fears out of my life and once again, the fear left in a very similar manner to the fear of dentists and hospitals. I performed my task with no fear and got 3 standing ovations. From that point on whenever I spoke to a large audience, I did it with ease and my faith rose to do many things I hadn't seen done before, like healing the sick, casting out demons and seeing many miracles happen.

Faith needs to be unfettered so that with boldness we speak the words God gives us and that in turn sees many miraculous things happen. I've seen epilepsy healed, aches and pains disappear and stroke victims healed and many other miracles. There is no limit to the miraculous once fear is

Faith - The Working Factors

cleared away and faith takes its proper place in our lives.

Taking fear away from our thinking and having it removed from our characters allows the boldness necessary for Faith to thrive. We need also to understand that without arrogance and the bravado that is so often evidently not a social grace, we need to be bold. In fact scripture tells us to 'come boldly to God's throne and find mercy and grace in times of need'. Problem periods are such times when faith must come into its own and challenge the difficulties and issues with the inner strength of faith.

So faith is what we need, not fear.

Faith - The Working Factors

Chapter Six
Faith going public.

We often don't have the compassion we should have to meet people's needs but instead defer to not wanting to be seen to 'stick out in public'.

Not many people want to 'go public' with their faith. Now I fully understand that. I was once full of fear in doing things publically, I just wanted a quiet life and I didn't want my friends to know what I believed. I wanted a 'private' life, with no comebacks or anyone challenging what I believed. That was because, **1**. I wasn't sure enough about what I believed and **2**. I didn't want to get in hot water over my beliefs (fear). Well people react to what you say sometimes, they will see your reticence and fear and come back challenging you, especially if you're defensive over what you're saying. Lack of confidence in what you believe will allow others to 'shake you down', as they say.

But watch this for a moment: knowing that what God says is solid and reliable is paramount for all of us. We need assurance about what we know and believe. This is where what God says is SO

Faith - The Working Factors

important. Once you listen to His wisdom and see the *strength* of what He says, your boldness increases. Now be careful here, our boldness should be what it says it is, 'Bold' but arrogance is not one of God's ways and we can be in trouble if we take in the wrong things and shout about them.

Just look at a very important scripture about faith, "... Faith *comes* by hearing, and hearing by the word of God." Romans 10 verse 17. We get our new, quickened, enlivened faith, from God. **He** speaks it and **we** hear it. He speaks it to us with His faith and we hear it *enlivened* in our hearing. From that point on the words of God are alive in us and if we believe them and act on them, they go into action, just as though He spoke them verbally among us Himself…. And that is a very important factor in faith manifestation. If you are going to see God's words **do** things, you have to speak them with knowledge and with His power behind them.

Once we see the power in what God believes and we speak His words meaningfully with conviction and truth, anything that is normally impossible to mankind, can happen.

Faith - The Working Factors

Look at something Jesus said.... "If you have faith, you will say to this mountain, 'Be removed and cast into the sea, and it will obey you'".

Jesus picks on a huge item to remove with your faith. I often wondered, 'Why did Jesus pick on such a big thing to remove? Why did he not choose a smaller item and start us off slowly, building up our confidence bit by bit until we are up and running with it?' But then I realised that if we saw that Jesus is aiming our faith at the biggest possible problem, He is doing it to make us realise that ***anything*** can be done by faith if we believe. Take Job's life for an example: Few can deny that Job had a horrific life after satan went to work on him, leaving him childless, poorer, weaker, restless in his mind, etc. He took every major thing off Job that mattered to him. Yet when Job made the faith statement that he knew that God could do ***everything***, his faith spoke up and he was given far more than he had originally. His faith restored all that he lost and gave him more than he had previously. You see, our God doesn't think the way we do, He speaks faith things, words with power-to-create, in them.

Faith - The Working Factors

He clearly tells us, 'My ways are not your ways, neither are my thoughts, your thoughts'. God has better thinking, the core of what He thinks is altogether greater in strength and intelligence. God doesn't have weakness and flaws integral to his thoughts as we have. Satan hasn't corrupted His thinking as it has ours. So if you need to think better, you need God's thoughts and then you need to act on those thoughts as He speaks His thoughts. So the answer is to listen to what He says and then *do* what He says. Jesus says, 'He that hears my words and does them is like a man who builds his house on a rock. The storms will come and blow on the house but the house stands strong because the foundation is strong.

Doing what God says usually means us acting on what he says ***in public***. I would say, reading other scriptures, that we have to ***act*** out and for people to see what we believe. This is always the case, just look at salvation itself, "If you believe in your heart and ***confess with your mouth***, you **will** be saved". Believing God is good but speaking out loud what you believe actually causes salvation. It's not enough to think good in your mind, you

56

Faith - The Working Factors

have to speak it out and make it go public, *then* the concept becomes actual and is seen publicly.

Just knowing that the house will be better built on rock is not enough, you have to clear away the sand and then put your bricks and materials on the bedrock beneath to have a strong house.

Clearing away the bad ideas and building on God's good ideas is the way to build strong. Often people need to see our sand-clearing and us reaching down onto bedrock to set out our house foundation.

Faith, we could say, *needs to be more obvious.* Saying it will not only make what we believe public but will put *into action* the power of good thinking, namely faith.

Chapter 7
The 'Rules' of faith.

Maybe this chapter should be better called, 'The ***Rule*** of Faith'. For there is really only one. That is, that you should ***Believe***. Jesus said it to the ruler of a synagogue in Mark 5:38.... Read the short passage.....
'But overhearing what they said, Jesus said to the ruler of the synagogue, "<u>Do not fear</u>, **only** believe."' **Just believe!** Accept what God is and what He can do and ask Him for whatever you need. He has promised us, that if we ask we will receive.

To go back to the 'Image, likeness and Spirit' of God, we were given Faith as we were given all of our abilities and faculties by Him. ***Faith is not complicated***, it never should have been. So *why this book?* Why so many pages talking about faith? It's because of the things that have been put in our faith's way. We need to clear them out, un-complicate things, simplify things and clear the air, and ONLY believe!

Faith - The Working Factors

Clear the decks! Get rid of all the little clauses that satan has tried to put in our contract (our covenant) with the Almighty. All those 'things that make us think again instead of acting in power and confidence, knowing that what God says, *we can actually do*.

Put away the excuses and stand firmly believing.
I say, take out the trash and clear the rubbish, leave only the truth that Jesus spoke. Listen, when Jesus spoke, the angry storm stilled and peace followed, not only there in the boat but in that whole region, so much so, that when they reached the other side of the lake, a madman who terrorised the neighbourhood, came kneeling at His feet submissive and powerless.

'You see what faith does? It emphasises the words of God and what He wants to happen and speaks it into practice. *The rule* is to *believe it* and what's more don't let the words of God get out of your head until you see it happen. See now, that's what faith is. It's the <u>evidence</u> of the unseen things that people have hoped and believed for. They put their trust in something God said, believed it and earnestly hoped to get it. That's the route to faith,

Faith - The Working Factors

and faith is the substance of their hope that appears in reality. IF YOU believe, says Jesus (Mark 11:22.) If you "Have faith in God", you will pick on huge obstructive objects and tell them to move out of your sight….. *And they will obey you*. He cites a mountain for an example.

The rule of faith is that no matter what the item is, whether it's huge or immovable by any means, whether it's a terminal sickness or an impossible situation that you cannot see a way out of, *believe God*. God can do what no one else can do and move the immovable.

The rule of faith is that no matter what Satan puts in your way to try and make life hell for you, you just believe that God has a way out of it. He always had a remedy to take His children out of harm's way. See now, there are no evil surprises for His children, - those who **know Him** and **trust Him** and *believe what He says*.

Faith operates via our communication system. Either we speak faith or we transmit it as it were by physical means. Let's look then at the verbal way for a moment. *Firstly, on a simple level*, if

Faith - The Working Factors

we are not aware of there being a faith to use when in need or in danger or whatever, then we learn wrongly that there is nothing to help us and continue to live that way, helpless. But if we listen to people who have actually done things by faith, we see a very different story entirely. Of course it's more complex than that but Faith must always be kept simple in its concept. Ordinary, even unlearned people use and exercise their faith once they know about it. God did not make it complicated and put it out of our reach, far from it. He makes it so simple, even little children operate in faith and see miracles happen if they believe it. Some of the young people in the Bible operated with great faith so it doesn't need a super-experienced person or a mature adult or a very intelligent person to operate in faith, just one who believes what God enables us to do. In fact as Jesus said to that one person quite simply, '**Only believe**'…..

I see this as a major aid to us seeing our faith operate well. JUST believe, forget the complicated doctrines and clauses that satan would try and write into our contract with God regarding faith. <u>Only believe</u>, keep it simple, trust God to do

Faith - The Working Factors

what He said He would do and simply believe. I could end the book there really, if you just go this far, it's enough, God does what He promises and we need always to remember that, otherwise satan, the world and our flesh will talk us out of believing. But just believe, God simply wants that trusting belief in His integrity, to exist in us, everything else is extra and usually not necessary. Many believers don't get that it's so simple, Jesus said, "A little child shall lead them".

So why this book then? 'Good question'. As I've said, we could end it right here. So this is for those of us who have been 'talked out of using faith' or have been told that there isn't any faith to be had or have been brought up being told, 'Christianity is all nonsense' or 'there is no God to help us' etc. In this vein we will speak later of incidents where God has done all sorts of things and refute the 'No God' notion from simple faith actions and outcomes. The book is also to show how that removing doubt is important to get faith working and dispelling unbelief, is also a factor. I remember a famous preacher was praying for the sick and one gentleman in the prayer line told him his complaint but added, 'But the doctor said it

Faith - The Working Factors

can't be cured'. The preacher replied 'But God can heal that.', to which the man replied several times, 'But the doctor said....' So the preacher said, "In the end I just went over his head and told the sickness to go and the man was immediately healed". The man jumped up and down in excitement and then exclaimed, "But the doctor said....." Believe God not men (or women).

We have a great catalogue available to us to show how faith works. The Bible is a tremendous text book on these things. God never expects us to just out-of-the-blue believe. He simply leads us to believe and encourages us with maybe small examples perhaps first, then grows our confidence until we're fully up and running and past our doubt.

Can I tell you of my own 'start up experience' with faith? I was always brought up to go to church and Sunday School. In Sunday School we were taught the stories of the Bible. Remember though that the Bible is a history book and not a story book in the sense of it being full of fictional tales.

Faith - The Working Factors

I remember hearing how young David the shepherd boy slew Goliath, the Philistine giant. None of the soldiers of the Israeli army wanted to engage with this huge man, even their tallest men backed down from facing him. But David, a boy with faith was angered by seeing great men back down when he was taking cheese to his brothers at the battlefield. Instead of being afraid, and letting it make him cower like everyone else, David instead felt righteously angry and ran towards the giant with his sling shot declaring that his God would slay the Philistine and that David would remove his head. David realised that the God that helped him guard the sheep from wolves and bears would also guard him from a giant. He did what he believed he could do with God's help. And kill the giant he did!

Now as a child I had developed asthma from age seven and spent many nights unable to breathe with the complaint. As I lay in bed one night, I remembered what the Bible said, 'Those that call on the name of God will be saved'. As I wheezed and coughed that night, I decided to call on God to help me. I began to speak the name of Jesus, to call on Him for help. It eased my breathing as I

Faith - The Working Factors

said the name 'Jesus'. As I did so, another voice spoke up and said, 'Aaah, if you say any word like that rhythmically it will help, so I thought of a very similar word and spoke that, I said the word, 'cheeses'. The bad breathing came back just as bad as before but the name Jesus relieved my breathing difficulty (remember, I was young and unlearned).

Now if you look at that example, you will see that I *heard* about faith firstly, *then* I acted on what the Bible said, which as a child I was told was 'God's words' and my faith *came alive* as I acted on it. It was often that I acted again against the accursed Asthma but whenever I did, with the life of God's words acting as a catalyst to my faith, the night Asthma stopped immediately and I began to sleep all night, every night without fail. I have in fact never lost a night's sleep since because of it.

So there's the pattern, ***the rule*** for active faith right there; ***we hear, we respond and act on what we hear*** and **faith works.** It did for me every time, every night without fail.

Faith - The Working Factors

God doesn't lie, He is truth itself; you can fully trust Him. Whenever I have ***seriously*** taken hold of what He says and used His words to take on a problem, it happens, whatever I asked for, I got.

So let's recapitulate then: If you ***hear*** what God says to do and ***act*** on it, faith becomes ***act***ive and your problem, whatever it is you are tackling, is dealt with.

I can relay so many instances of when my faith, which in the beginning, I didn't know I had, worked fine. I will relay many of these later in this book. In fact the stories are essential, it's how faith is born in others, by hearing of what happened when someone believed and acted. This is really what the Bible is saying, that 'faith comes (active) from hearing and hearing (faith testimonies) by the word of God'. The means to realise that the impossible or the necessary can be done when you hear someone say that it can happen and you believe what they say. Even in the normal, natural world this is so. Someone will tell you one day that if you make wings with such and such a shape and add them to a plane fuselage, the plane will fly given the right conditions, with thrust etc. You may not believe them but if you

Faith - The Working Factors

listen more, the rest of the information will prove it right to you and the plane will fly. The end result, the flying plane, *is* faith, it's the **substance** of what you believed for **or hoped** for. Hebrews 11 verse 1.

Listen a moment to what Jesus said in Mark chapter 11, "If you have faith, you will say to this mountain, 'Be removed and cast into the sea, and it will obey you". A tall order? Yes, to our upbringing, in our 'normal' thinking, in this world, it can't be done but not impossible if it needs to be done. Listen to something else Jesus says.... "With God all things *are* possible" and then He adds, "If *you* believe, all things *are* possible". There's the method of getting faith to work again, right there. 1. Hear what Jesus says to activate your faith, then 2. Act and it happens. Most of us know that God can do anything, what we often fail to realise is that if we are made in His Image and likeness, then *we* have that ability to do the normally impossible as well.

Now I realise that there are many factors that prevent us easily believing that, which is why I have written this book. Let's just look at one

Faith - The Working Factors

factor in brief, we will deal with it again later but consider your first step out in faith. You hear what Jesus says you can do with your faith and you are say, like the disciples were, in a storm on the seas and the boat is beginning to capsize. Jesus stood up in the boat when they woke Him and said to the storm, "Peace, Be still" and the wind and waves obeyed him. Your feelings would be, 'Will the storm respond to me speaking, like it did to Jesus speaking?' Now your faith has to answer that question but if you know that what Jesus says always happens and is true, then the wind and waves will stop.

At home on one occasion not long after we moved to our house, we were experiencing very high winds, such that they were ripping heavy concrete tiles off the roof and they were smashing as they hit the driveway below. This was expensive and labour intensive to repair and the winds were happening often. It was a real nuisance. I got angry about it after a while. We have a three-storey house and it's high to climb up there, it has to be done on very long ladders.

Faith - The Working Factors

One day as yet another storm began, my anger rose again, I could see pieces already starting to come off the roof and tree branches also coming down. In my righteous anger I went to the front door and opened it. I stood on the porch steps and yelled at the storm with words like Jesus used, **"Peace!** *Be still*, - enough of this!" Within just about 5 minutes the storm had stopped. It was all quiet again. Was it me that did it, no, it was God but He responded to my faith. God will always act when you use your faith.

Ok sometimes our faith does not seem to work, often because we are fearful. Fear inhibits our faith but we will talk too about how fear stops our faith and how we can live a life of confidence and dispense with fear. Sufficient to say for the moment though is the realisation that many things either prevent faith from ever starting up or limit our use of it but we can remedy those things by rooting out the causes. We will also deal with these things in this book.

So let's resume speaking about how faith is installed or should I say, 're-commissioned' because it is already there. Most of us didn't

Faith - The Working Factors

realise it. We hear and the words that talk of faith tell us firstly that we all have it, whether we realise it or not and then hearing is the main route by which we see how we use the faith that we have. "Faith comes by hearing and hearing by the word of God" is how the Bible puts it. It is not unusual to have abilities we didn't know we had, let's not forget, we learn to do many things in life that we had no idea we could do.

But the overall number one rule that is above all else is that we believe. <u>We put trust and complete confidence in what God says is true and put it above all else that is said.</u> All that appears in front of us, appearing to be right, if it opposes what God says, then it's false, in some way or another. The secret of faith is that it is based in absolute truth, in what God believes. His Spirit sees the actual and possible, whereas we see only part of what's possible or what exists before us.

We must know that we only ever see part of the problem, there is also the spiritual, unseen side of things to account for. We can often miss seeing the spiritual aspect of situations. ***Let me show you an illustration from scripture:***

Faith - The Working Factors

Jesus is on the lake in the boat with the disciples and they are 'Going to the other side' of the lake. On the other side of the lake is a man who is very troubled in his mind and spirit and is basically terrorising the neighbourhood. The demons inside him are scaring everyone by their ferocity etc. He has been chained up many times by the local community but the demon power in him simply breaks the chains. I can imagine children being called indoors out of the man's way for their safety. So it's Jesus' mission that day to set the man free.

Now look at the background of the area. This place where they are going to is the country of the Gadarenes ('Gergasenes' in Hebrew). If we go back in time, this was the Gergasene tribe, one of many that Joshua had so much trouble with. They were wicked and aggressive towards Israel. The demons in the man were of that culture and aggression. He would cut himself with sharp stones and knives and live among the tombs.

As Jesus and the disciples crossed the lake towards this area and consequently towards the man,

Faith - The Working Factors

scripture tells us, 'An ***angry*** storm arose' such that the winds were 'scooping up the water and throwing it into the boat'. The 'anger' of the storm was trying to sink their boat and prevent Jesus and the disciples from reaching the area and the man and also the demonic forces territorial to the area. Jesus, who was asleep all this time in the back of the boat, was woken by the disciples who were very fearful and scared. 'Don't you care that we perish?' they asked Jesus in their panic.

Jesus came to the centre of the boat and stood there and spoke to the situation. "Peace, be still", He commanded. The winds and the waves stood still and the angry waters calmed down.

As they came to the far shore, the demoniac came running to Jesus, submissive and kneeling, subservient and under control. Jesus then cast out the demons and took control of the whole of the man's situation. The man then sat at peace and 'in His right mind', just like the storm. The community's worries were over. PEACE came to the whole area.

Faith - The Working Factors

Note that when Jesus dealt with the storm the man became subservient and peaceful and more, when Jesus cast out the spirits of that nation and area. The background of the man's troubles came from the territory of that place which was occupied by so many spirits, which we know the history of, from Joshua's dealings with it.

Often people are under wrong spiritual influence having been brought up in areas where certain sin and evils have been practiced but faith and the power of faith are the answer to all these problems.

In this case, a whole community's problems were 'fixed' by faith so that peace could reign.

I also want you to see the things Jesus said about both **faith** and **fear** here. After He stilled the storm and calmed the area, including the demoniac, He turned to the disciples and asked them, "How is it that you have so ***little*** Faith… and why do you have such ***great*** fear?" There are two things to note here: 1. That fear and faith are related by the area they occupy within us. 2. The ratio of faith to fear is important to notice.

Faith - The Working Factors

We can't have both faith and fear. They come from different sources. Fear comes from satan. Faith comes from God. God relayed the information to me one day in personal revelation. He said, 'Fear is knowing what satan can do to you, Faith is knowing what I can do for you'.

Fear will make you cower and run away. Faith will cause you to stand bold when things get scary. We need to contemplate the differences between the two. Satan will always muddle things and try and make the two indistinct but really they are so different, like chalk and cheese. The secret is to know the difference and segregate them, shunning fear at every point and grasping God's words and using faith at every opportunity. This is how we GROW.

Faith - The Working Factors

Chapter Eight
Putting Hope back where it should be.

A big part of Faith being operative is the factor that brings it into being. Hope is the initiator that we have to have before any success initiative can be put into practice.

In Romans 8 we read, "We are saved by Hope".... Probably one of the most underestimated and downgraded attributes we have is hope.

The word 'Hope' has become a negative in many people's minds. We can all recall people who, trying to be nice, many of them just religious and not faith believers, speaking the old cliché in a negative and really not very meaningful way, "Well... I *hope* you'll be better soon". We all know that there is no hope in the saying in this context. The trouble with hearing it said so many times without a faith content either in the phrase or in the person, it adds nothing, in fact it becomes the opposite. We find, on hearing it, its as though the speaker has given up on hope and is just trying to sound pious. The word has become downgraded and meaningless in a lifeless way.

Faith - The Working Factors

<u>This is not Hope.</u> ***Hope is a lively, expectant and demanding thing in reality.*** It brings us from a feeling of destitution, to having visions of a lively future ahead and saves us from an abyss of nothingness. Hope is a power to take us from an utter feeling of failure to a knowledge that somehow we can overcome any trial or loss. Hope is God's special tool to make us see a future triumph when we have nothing to base our optimism on. It's a resurrection experience seen in advance, a victory that no one else can see perhaps except you, a feeling of future security when all is at sea and lost.

Hope is powerful. It's like a pick me up, a tonic that lifts your soul, or at least should be. Hope makes a way forward in your mind when the sight in front of you is blocked. **HOPE must be redefined if we are to get the best out of our faith.**

There is too little hope in the world, especially in the minds of people who have no knowledge of God and who He is, to pick them up and lift their hearts when things have so often proved themselves to be pessimistic and fruitless. In real

Faith - The Working Factors

terms people without God can't see a future very often and that's a situation too common and should never have been.

The Bible says, "We are born in sin (rebellion against God and all that is good) and shaped by iniquity (unfairness and injustice).

But God never made us with these attitudes and attributes, He made us with ***hope.*** He gave us His own image, His lively imagination that can see us out of every dead end and failing. God gave us a Spirit that has life in it so powerful that when death is all around us, it lives on in optimism. Just like you can't kill light with darkness, you can't kill life itself because God is life.

We need to remember that as Adam set us on the path of rebelling against all that God is, we all have some weaknesses built into our optimism and ability to see our way out of despair.

To remedy the loss that sits in our souls and overcome the feeling of despair and often desperation, God gives us salvation. He provides it when Jesus dies and is resurrected and provides

Faith - The Working Factors

a new way out in our vision to replace the feelings of negativity and hope-lessness.

Without the resurrection of Jesus ever having come into our thinking, the possibility of us ever rising out of our 'problem-states', never occurs to us. ***But God in raising Jesus from the dead puts out an idea to us that nothing else can provide us with,*** a future, when there is no future. That's called HOPE.

Hope precedes victory. We see the glimmer of light at the end of the tunnel as we say. We coined that phrase to describe hope. When everything is closed around us and dark, we can see the way out and the light at the end of the tunnel. It's a good metaphor. But hope is more. Hope says there IS an answer. There IS a remedy, there is a real and communicable outlook that is good.

The resurrection of Jesus is the key to all hope as were the words of God from the prophets in the times before that. There has to be a preceding statement or vision of a way out before we can see an expectation of the help we need.

Faith - The Working Factors

Just think for a moment. We all think of death as the end and we also are all aware that it will come to us at some time. If *only* that thought existed in our minds, we would not have any concept of a real way out of situations. But just for a moment think about Jesus' resurrection. All of a sudden there is always a way out once you consider that ***the most final and complete finish to a life, is reversible.*** Of course the answer is in the Spirit of God. He is life, there is no death in Him. So when there is a dead-end situation with no solution to it, the answer is in the Spirit of God. He has initiatives that no one else has, hence the saying of Jesus that 'With God all things are possible'. But to consider this further, Jesus then said, 'If you believe, all things are possible', so if you want a remedy for something that can't be done, God's Spirit in you will provide the remedy and raise a hope to make it happen. This is hope in the real sense. Not a cliché that it *might* be possible or *may* provide some sort of answer to help but a ***real, vital, actual solution***.

This is of course all part of the 'renewing of our minds' that is possible to the believer. We read the words of God with limited understanding and

Faith - The Working Factors

God's Spirit enlightens us with a new remedy or a new initiative. After all, the Holy Spirit is the one who raised Jesus from the dead, He is the one we want in a 'dead' situation. He is *exactly* the one, the *only* one to do the job, who **can** do the job.

So I want you to see that when it comes to the notion of 'hope', the true author of hope is God Himself. When there *is* no way out, there actually now is, *because* Jesus rose over death and that means that whatever problem is normally insurmountable, now it isn't any more.

This is a ***big*** theme. It spreads across ***all*** problems of ***all types***. Once you realise the principle here that the Holy Spirit is the gateway to answering any and all problems, the SKY's the limit. We haven't often in our churches spoken in this way and there's a reason for this because not all believers see the full truth of God's promises. It's often because the subject of hope and resulting faith is not understood because many churches, though seeing the principle of the resurrection of Jesus, don't fully believe it and accept it.

Faith - The Working Factors

Salvation is the old person being 'born-again'. The new start in life is actually brought about by the Holy Spirit injecting life into us, if you like, - causing our own resurrection. So whether we realise it or not, the Spirit of ultimate hope is inside us. So what is it that you hope for? Freedom from your old ways? Freedom from your old sicknesses? Do you need new abilities to innovate and have initiatives? Is there a problem in your life that you have never surmounted?

Well the answers to all problems and issues are within you. The Holy Spirit resident in us after salvation and baptism is right where you need Him, ***inside you.*** And He is hope, lively hope, not dead or false hope but living, bright hope that actually leads us to real answers.

Chapter Nine
The Holy Spirit – 'The God in you' Factor

For all our problems to be solved, the best remedy is to have the *master solver* with you at all times. In John chapter 14, we read that Jesus promises us a 'helper', the 'comforter' as He is called. This *is* the Holy Spirit. Notice what Jesus calls Him. He calls the Holy Spirit a 'helper', which is what we all need from time to time inside us to solve our problems and provide, 'on-board' help. The original Greek word used and translated 'helper' and 'comforter' is the Greek word 'Parakletos'. The word means 'one who stands beside you to console'. To show yet another factor in our faith journey, I want to highlight the Holy Spirit's nearness when we need Him.

God never meant us to be helpless at any time. Adam and Eve were given total dominion in the earth immediately after their creation. God breathed into Adam and Eve the breath of life. For me, that's the Holy Spirit undoubtedly and the Holy Spirit in His fullness. The Dominion came from God's presence within them, He is the

Faith - The Working Factors

Almighty and they were made in His Image and Likeness.

After salvation, after we are forgiven for our rebellion and now have the ability to 'house' God's Spirit, who will give us back dominion as we learn His ways and are taught by Him. Jesus said that the Holy Spirit is also our 'counsellor' who will teach us all things.

So look at the provision that our Heavenly Father makes for us such that we never have a need again. We are made in His Image and Likeness and filled with His helper.

Recently I saw a new 'vision, as it were of the Helper, the Parakletos. 'Parakletos', being the one standing alongside us, I saw His Spirit as it were, inside us, right up against our Spirit, embracing our spirit closely, teaching us how to use our faith and overcome our problems.

To me, this is precisely how God intends to help us to live, if we let Him. Most Pentecostal believers who invite the Holy Spirit into their lives have experienced the indwelling power and help of

Faith - The Working Factors

God's Spirit, stimulating their faith, teaching them how to believe the best way and how to deny satan and overcome sin and wrong. Salvation, if it is anything is God furnishing us with power to live fully and freely and not be contained by sin, fear or any evil.

I want to just put in a point here. God is not here to tyrannically dominate us. He made us with a free will and will never to overrule us. We were made exactly like Him, therefore we get a totally free but powerful life. We are not robots but living, breathing, free people, made wonderfully in body and soul and spirit and filled with God's life. *His* Spirit is then alongside *our* spirit which is being 'coached' on how to live victoriously.

We should never be downtrodden or sick or weak or prisoners to anyone. Being a child of God means we have the top status and privileges always intended for us.

It's not until you look carefully into scripture like Genesis 1 and 2 that you see who we should be and how we should act in the light of it. Reading the words of God makes us realise that we should

Faith - The Working Factors

be having dominion where nothing puts us down.
Look! The Bible often says 'behold'. There's a load of hidden stuff that we should 'see' that will give us a lively and powerful hope that drives us to a faith that works every time.

We talk of the resurrection of Jesus but until we become associated as it were with the reality of it and it gets mixed into our system and we see it properly as a real, *life giving* experience, it can remain a remote and dull event. But resurrection is far from dull, it is a remarkable and scintillating event that removes all your doubt about the impossible happening. It moves your thinking into an entirely new experience of life with the emphasis of the subject of **life** being the centre of it.

The Holy Spirit IS the life, He IS the power of life and the vitality of it. He breathed into Adam to ***make him*** a ***living*** soul.

When you need life and not death or you need a live situation instead of a dead and worthless situation, or you need a solution to a problem that you have no solution to, it's God's Spirit you need.

Faith - The Working Factors

God's super intelligence, His 'know how' is all powerful, after all, He created the universe so again 'look', 'behold', who we're dealing with. The resurrection precedes the coming of the Holy Spirit to us. It's fitting, Jesus rose out of death that troubled everyone and then gave *us* the Spirit that rose *Him* up. Listen, I mean the *same* Spirit that rose Jesus from the dead is the one who makes *us* alive and 'quickens' *us,* as the Bible puts it (Romans 8 verse 11).

Even looking at the old English we can see that the things that were slow and un-lively are made rapid and lively by God's Spirit. **And these are all relevant to our faith, in fact, MAJOR factors.** So invite the Holy Spirit into your life and be 'quickened', - made alive in all of your being. Adam's living being, his soul, was all powerful in the earth, he had dominion over everything. Now *this* is the existence God intended and *still intends* for us.

Being faith believers is what all Christians should be, filled with God's Spirit and acting with their God given faith. We need to get the restraints and

Faith - The Working Factors

<u>the doubts off our lives</u> so that we become what He wants us to be, ***ALIVE in every sense***.

So hope starts with the indwelling spirit of God, with what God says and what He is. And faith follows with the substance of what we hoped for, with the evidence of what we couldn't previously see. God is amazing.

Chapter Ten
Freedom, the moving forward factor.

So we're establishing a picture of faith and its work and also seeing what else may be needed to make our faith more active.

We've said that we need hope before we can bring faith into action. We have also said that all hope is derived from God and His Spirit of resurrection. It's also seen in previous chapters that fear and faith don't mix, you have to ditch one to get the other and that works both ways. To get fear, you have to remove faith but far more importantly, you have to ditch fear to let your faith really motor. Living through a fear experience and 'sticking to your guns' as we say, believing what God says about a matter, destroys fear. We walk through the valley of all that normally makes us fearful and we trust God all the way through that valley. We then emerge victorious and free from the fear that we had in that environment. I can testify of quite a few situations where fear came out of me when I stood for right-ness and withstood evil. Even when I was very fearful in those situations, after standing firm believing God, fear got up and left, I

Faith - The Working Factors

heaved and retched it out of me. It just up and left once firmly challenged. And sometimes it works in other ways too.

I remember a famous singer who became a Christian believer, but she was once a heavy smoker. She one day made a promise to God after being convinced that smoking was not good, that she would never touch another cigarette. The effect was to cause an awful repulsion within her and she vomited a horrible black tarry substance and she then felt 'such a freedom' and a clean feeling.

So there are many things that help us to clean up our lives and take us out of dark places so that we can live free with no fears and restraints. **God wants us free.**

The problem, (another faith 'factor') often involved here is that we need to see that God not only wants us free but has set up the means to free us. Whether to set us free from sin, sickness, fear, dread, poverty, weakness, difficulty, despair, pain,

Faith - The Working Factors

and all the other things that could be against you. Take a moment to think of the biggest problem in your life and realise that there is a way out.

Putting aside the wrong understanding and seeing that with God all things are possible, is not only good to learn but works at many levels. We *do* need to believe however but when belief seems to elude you, realise that you were never on your own. Many have been there, including people in the scriptures. People from Jonah in the old testament to a man whose son was an epileptic in the new testament had problems believing. Jesus asked the man, "Do you believe I can do this?" The man replied, "Lord I believe, *but help my unbelief".* Jesus complied and healed his son. You see, unbelief is something many of us have but asking God to help us in our situation is the right way forward. *God always wants us moving forward with faith,* not backwards but always forwards, not regressing into fear and retreating into inability but moving forwards with help from His Spirit, learning that if *we* believe *all things are possible.*

Faith - The Working Factors

Notice that, with young David facing Goliath the Philistine giant, he didn't run from him but after proclaiming that he would remove the giants head, he ran towards him and spoke in faith. David realised that this giant had no covenant with God - but David did. Do you see? You can bring factors into your problem area that assists your faith. It's called 'believing the truth and trusting God' against all odds. We can help ourselves or allow difficulty to obstruct our way forward.

Just look at 1 John 3:20-22 NKJV
Let's knock out another objection that can be raised against us, that we are condemned by satan and sin etc…. Look at what God does for us…
"***For if our heart condemns us***, God is greater than our heart, and knows all things. [21] Beloved, if our heart does not condemn us, we have confidence toward God. [22] **And whatever we ask, we receive from Him,** because we keep His commandments and do those things that are pleasing in His sight."

Did you see it? *If we believe*, God overlooks our condemnation because Jesus died for us to remove the stuff that stops us seeing our faith work.

Faith - The Working Factors

Whatever we ask of Him, we receive. We have confidence towards God, if we realise we are not condemned and we simply ask and we get. Just do those things that are pleasing to him.

We can either accept the factors that satan tries to put in front of us to stop us living in faith or we reject them. Either we *let* our hearts condemn us even though we are forgiven by God or *we don't* take the thought and instead exclaim, "**I am not the condemned**, *I am the free, set free from the law of sin and death and I'm liberated by the law of the Spirit of life in Christ Jesus*". We need to clear the way before us and believe that we can ask anything of God and receive it.

There are many things we are free from once we are born again but we must realise them. Here's an example: Our new creation doesn't know what fear is because it's born of God. God doesn't have fear, *you can't scare him.* He's the Almighty, why would He have fear? Well, we *are* born again *of His Spirit*.

I developed a saying after God prompted me, '**God is bigger than you think** and if you are made in

Faith - The Working Factors

His image and likeness and filled with His Spirit, ***then YOU are bigger than you think'***. We have to stop thinking despairingly, we are not that person we were and this is a faith factor too! It's satan's desire to pull us down in our thinking and if he can do that then we will always lose but if we see who we are, we will always run towards the giants and not run away from them. We *have* the upper hand, its God's hand in Heaven backing us and it lifts us up and promotes us. 'I can do all things through Christ who strengthens me'. We are, 'Strengthened with all might in the inner man'. There are so many scriptures that tell us how strong we are with God in us. We are bigger than we think. As long as we 'think' about who we now are we will be better and stronger people.

Can I just put something in perspective? We must not forget humility with all our strong standing in God. I like a phrase from ... 1 Peter 5:6 NKJV 'Therefore humble yourselves under the mighty hand of God, that He may exalt you in due time'. See now, we don't need arrogance and the bravado of satan, we need humility, that gentle power of Spirit like God has. I always say, we need to have humility not humiliation. Satan humiliates us if

Faith - The Working Factors

we follow his ways but God gives us power *with* humility. Many try to defeat satan with his own tools. Let me tell you they are not good tools. God gives us cool, solid authority that our belief system uses to the full if we utilise it.

So to recapitulate, let's gather the factors a bit and put the beliefs together. We need hope to base our beliefs upon. That hope must come from the Holy Spirit, from God inside us. The Spirit of God in us will resurrect us out of every hard and evil situation because He was the one who raised Jesus from the dead, He has the ability. We need to build ourselves up in the most holy faith, remember we have God's faith in us. God's faith will cause us to run *at* the giants *not away from them*. We are not losers, we are winners, *that's* what God made us. Show me anyone in the Bible who lost out while they put their faith in God.

The Bible is given us for a reason. To make us think strong and the Bible itself tells us, 'As a man thinks, so he is. So thinking strong and clearly is paramount.

Faith - The Working Factors

Chapter Eleven
Doubt, The disabling factor

We have spoken about Hope having the resurrection as its origin power. We spoke of belief and overcoming and many positive things that contribute to a lively hope and a well-founded belief system. But now we need to tackle the things that stand in the way of belief for *all things* to be possible. For all things to be possible, there has to be no doubt, *then* we have no obstacles in our way. We need our belief unfettered and free to see the impossible actually done. So let's look at one or two of the things that try to negate belief and stand in its way.

Firstly, DOUBT. The origin of the word is '*double*'. That gives us a clue as to why we need rid of doubt. There's only *one* thing we need in our thinking *and that's clean pure belief.* So we need rid of any 'other' belief we have that stands opposed to us believing for good to happen.

Double-mindedness is the same thing. We need rid of the second(ary) belief and only accept the one true promise of God, that if we believe Him,

Faith - The Working Factors

nothing doubting, we will have what we are believing for. It's not rocket science. This is better than rocket science!

Second beliefs are not good. A primary belief is focused on just one thing and has only one view of a thing. We should always have a proper view of things so that we can't be misled or seduced into believing wrong.

But there are so many contradictions in the world today. Some of them are obvious but even the common sayings are becoming contradictory. I had a friend who had been to a great worship service. He told me, "It was wicked". I pulled him up about what he said. I said, "I thought you meant it was good!" He said that it *was* good, but I said, "But you said it was 'wicked'. Was it wicked or good?" "It was good of course", he said.

Look, if we can't get our words right how can we get our faith and our beliefs right? We need to be single minded and not mixing up our speech because speech is what we use to define what we want and need. Having two minds about

Faith - The Working Factors

something means that we aren't sure about it. We think one thing but if there's something else messing with our thinking that causes doubt, we need to ditch the thought and 'rightly divide the truth' as scripture tells us.

So many Christian believers have never thought out some of the things that confuse them; they need to analyse them to find the real truth.

Here's a common confusion among believers. "I don't know if it's God's will to heal me" they say. Now come on, look at the evidence in scripture, why would God want His creation, His sons and daughters sick? Why would He walk among us healing all that were sick and oppressed and not want us healed? *Of course it's His will to heal us.* Look at the leper that came to Jesus. He said to Jesus, Lord *if you will*, you **can** make me well. Jesus said categorically, "*I will*, be healed!" There's God's will right there. So never doubt it again.

So is it God's will to always get us out of trouble then? **Yes,** *of course* He wants you safe. You're His child. Of course He wants His children safe.

Faith - The Working Factors

So cry out to Him for help and expect help to come. "But I can't see how He can help me!," you say. That doesn't matter, you're in trouble, so ask for help from your Father in Heaven and *expect help*. See now, we need to clear out the confusion. The great verse in John's gospel says it all, "For God **so** loved the world He gave His only begotten son, that *whoever believed on him* should **not perish** but have everlasting life." He wants to save you. How often? ALWAYS. HE **WANTS** TO HEAL YOU. HOW OFTEN? ALWAYS. Of how many sicknesses? - *ALL* OF THEM! The churches that erroneously preach that it's not always God's will to heal you, are double minded. Psalm 103, Says, "You forgive all our iniquities and heal all our diseases". It goes on… "You redeem our life from destruction and crown us with loving kindness and tender mercies." Does that sound like a God who's dubious about whether he loves us or doesn't know if He wants to bless us? *Of course not.* Let's get real and kick the doubt out. 'Other' speech is doubt talking.

It's not God who's doubtful about whether we should be blessed with forgiveness and healing.

Faith - The Working Factors

It's us! So will His love last? Yes. "He loves us with an everlasting love". Read the word of God, the Bible, *properly*. You will see everywhere in it, **He loves us**. He *will* rescue us. He will deliver us from trouble always. Read Psalm 91 thoroughly. If you love Him, there's nothing He won't save you from. He'll give His angels charge over you to look after you in all your ways.

We have to get the rot out of our thinking. As Andrew Womack says so often, "Get rid of your stinking thinking". We come to a loving God who went through hell to save us, why do we think He would turn us away. "But God doesn't answer every prayer", you say. Well that's not what the Bible says. It's what *we* said. There's no contradiction in what God says, the contradiction is in us.

Do you see what I've done? I've taken the 'double-ness' out of the equation and left only one thought, that 'God is **for** us'. He is not against us. He will heal our hearts, our thoughts, our bodies, our situations, simply because **He *is* a healer.** He will release us from our sins and iniquities simply because He's a **forgiver**. I admit that often we

Faith - The Working Factors

need to change for some things to happen. Jesus said, "If you don't forgive, your Father in Heaven will not forgive you." <u>So forgive</u>, get the weakness out of the system and feel the comfort and ease of forgiveness in your soul. God is the great forgiver, He loves to forgive and set people free, all He asks is equity, that we forgive others too. Now see, *that* is double mindedness, if we don't forgive but want forgiveness ourselves, - we're really being double minded.

Double standards are the curse of society. Good, reliable people however, are the salt of the earth.

Don't let your mind be confused, God is good, ***always.*** Don't allow people to tell you that sometimes He's this and then sometimes, he's that. One indefatigable thing about God is that He never changes, He's always good, always righ and He always blesses right-ness.

Don't be half hearted, be full hearted, let goodness reign in you. Don't have double standards, having right standards makes you strong in character.

Faith - The Working Factors

The '***doub**le*' in '***doub**t*' kills our belief system. So let your whole mind be taken up with *believing* God. When you need to be healed, Jesus says, "**Only** believe!" Let any other thoughts go and *just* believe.

Destroy the doubter in you by only believing and let the unbelief go. It's like saying, "destroy the weakness in you by being strong and let the weakness go.
Alternatively, let the darkness go and let the light shine in you. Believe God and let satan's thoughts go unheard or unheeded. They're no good to you.

In the gospels Jesus says, 'take no thought for tomorrow, tomorrow will take thought for itself'. Well sometimes we need to not take a thought about something. It's when satan or our flesh or the world suggests something that we know is not useful to us or good for us, we need to ignore it, to take no thought for it. It's a good practice to ignore what we know to be useless to us.

Be single minded, just take right-ness, build a good life, don't doubt, just believe God.

Faith - The Working Factors

And here's another thing…. You can't be fearful and be calm. Ditch the fear and then be calm and sure. ***You can't be both***. Single minded, believing one thing, one right attitude is the simple way, God's way. Get away from the complicated, convoluted thinking of confusion and fear and keep a calm mind based on God's peace and His truth. And don't back down.

Backing down from believing is doubt in action its ***un***-belief. Believe what Jesus said and 'only believe.' We have no cause to back down, God is behind everything we do when we do what He says in faith. Backing down should not be a factor in our lives. I so like the attitude of Caleb and Joshua when they go with the other 10 to spy out the promised land. They *all* see giants in this land and the 10 back down but Caleb and Joshua just declare 'We *can* go up and take this land' (forget the giants, God will take care of the giants).

Doubt comes in many forms but we know doubt, we feel the negativity of it, that uncertainty, that subtle shutting down of our confidence and our faith. Defeat it, knock it down, destroy it with God's words. 'Only believe!'

Chapter Twelve
The results of faith

I have often preached a sermon (if you would like to call it that) around the world. When I am in Africa, Pastor Michael Mandali will often ask me, "Will you preach it today?" I have often preached, 'With God all things are possible' and proceeded to tell of testimonies of people who have seen many miracles, that *prove* that very fact.

As I preach and tell the stories of what people have seen happen, the audience receive the message and then the new testimonies start; "As you were speaking yesterday, the pains that I have had in my back for years just disappeared." "As you spoke and prayed on the radio last evening, all my stomach pain disappeared". As you were reaching this evening, the pains that have racked my body all day, just went and have not returned!" One mother phoned us as we travelled on to another venue to tell us, 'My son's epilepsy has *gone*'.

When I got home to the UK following a 3 week mission in Uganda, I had an email from the principal of a secondary school. It read, "Dear

Faith - The Working Factors

Pastor Terry, that was such a powerful message you preached on Sunday morning to the school, so we gave an appeal for those who wanted salvation (I had simply prayed over the school pupils and committed them all to the Lord before rushing off and running up the road to preach at another church at eleven o'clock and had not made a formal appeal to them for salvation) I want to tell you that the whole school gave their lives to Jesus today!" We are talking about over 200 pupils!

My responses to these testimonials are usually, "Really?" It always (pleasantly) surprises me to hear of a miracle God has done. He's just amazing.

I visited Uganda again one year after preaching at a little village called Busea. The previous year I had preached in a little church there and on arrival was shown to the Pastor's house being told that he was ill in bed and had suffered a stroke. When I went into the house, he was in bed and all of his left side was paralysed. His face had dropped on the left side too and he was confined to bed unable to move himself.

Faith - The Working Factors

As I entered the church compound the following year, Pastor Mandali pointed out someone to me and asked me, "Do you know this gentleman?" I did recognise him somewhat but with some reservation. "'You remember you prayed for the Pastor last year?" Pastor Mandali asked. "Yes" I said, "Well this is him". I looked at the man up and down and there was no sign whatsoever of any stroke symptoms. He stood up straight and his left side was normal and so was his face, which had no droop at all to it. His left arm, though, was draped across his stomach as if it could be still problematic, so I asked, "Is your arm OK?" At this point he waved the arm enthusiastically in all directions. "It's fine", He said, and we all laughed and praised God.

As an addition to this miracle it was told me that since his healing from the stroke, the Pastor's ministry had so improved, the congregation has increased vastly in number. So much so, that they have had to extend the church in length. So while I was there, I gave the church some funds that were given to me as I left for Uganda that year. They already had the bricks stacked up at the back

Faith - The Working Factors

of the church so the funds paid for the cement and other materials. ***God has funds for everything***

Do I hang around and wait to see *if* God has healed all the people I've prayed for? ***No I don't.*** It isn't my business to see *if* God will heal them. He promised to heal them if I laid my hands on them so that's sufficient for me.

Do I see people healed instantly in front of me? No, not always but its great when we do see it.

Preaching at the Easter convention in Mbale town, Uganda one year, I was about to get up to preach and was waiting on the Holy Spirit for the 'lead-in' to the message, an opening phrase, if you like. The worship time had been amazing, you could sense God's presence everywhere in the large hall. The people were just 'glistening' with His presence. I stood at the rostrum and was very reluctant to begin my message. I just said, "I don't want to interrupt what God is doing here, let's just praise Him". Then God prompted me to challenge the congregation. "Place your hand on your body where you need healing, the Holy Spirit is here to heal you!" I saw many move their hands to

Faith - The Working Factors

various parts of their anatomy and many looked upwards in faith, to God. Then I asked for all those who had used their faith, to try and prove their healing by lifting the ailing part or exercising or whatever. I then asked for all those who could now do what they couldn't do before, to signal to me and hands went up all over the 2-3,000 congregation. People were jumping for joy and obviously now not in pain or disabled any more.

God can do anything He wants to do, He only needs someone to say what ***He*** wants to say, to guide people toward His truth, that 'He is the Lord that heals us' and sets us free from our problems.

Some say in a link with scripture that 'a prophet is not accepted in his own country'. For me this means that those living around us maybe don't see us as believers that have dynamic faith but don't be put off by the rumour mill of satan, if God tells you to do something, then do it.

I was away in Bletchley near London lecturing in midweek and travelling home for weekends. During one week my wife had told me in a phone call that she had a cold that seemed to be making

Faith - The Working Factors

her chest wheezy. On the Friday morning at our college I was helping tidy the workshops and preparing the lecture room ready for a new training course on the following Monday. As we worked, my boss came in to the room and told me to go home. My home was around 2 hours away and he said he didn't want me claiming overtime pay if I got home late. He insisted for some reason. So I soon left for home.

I therefore got home around 2 hours earlier than normal. As I drove down the driveway to the house, my son was running to meet me. "Come quick Dad", He said, "Mummy's in bed, she can't breathe and she's talking oddly!" I ran to the bedroom and found my wife Helen with noisy breathing and delirious. I had little time to get an ambulance or a doctor but went straight for the oil bottle that we used when we prayed for the sick.

Oil is the symbol of God's Spirit so I anointed her and prayed. "You sickness, in Jesus name be gone!" I said. In around 2 minutes she opened her eyes and was lucid in her speech. "What are you doing home so early?" she said, looking at the clock. It was just as well that I took my boss's instruction and came home early. If I had stayed in work, Helen would have died and I can't imagine what effect that would have had on my eleven year son Matthew. After a while I asked Helen what she wanted to do next, now that she was lucid and had her free will back. She decided after a while that she wanted to get the doctor. So we sent for our GP and when he arrived he looked extremely concerned. Helen's breathing was still noisy and after listening to her chest, the doctor called for an ambulance. "She has Pneumonia, she must go to hospital," He said.

While we waited for the ambulance, he repeatedly, at intervals, listened to her breathing and then paced the floor. At one point he stared out of the window with a searching expression on his face. "Is something wrong doctor?" I asked. "I don't understand it", he said. "I have seen pneumonia many times but I have never seen it getting better on its own before!"

God has His own way to confirm what He's done and we need to see what He's done with clarity.

Faith - The Working Factors

The great evangelist Oral Roberts came to my home city of Newport, Gwent UK many years ago, to hold a crusade preaching salvation and praying for the sick. So many people got born again and healed. I saw many jumping for joy at their healing and a man in a wheelchair got up and walk away from it. I didn't see the *many* others that got healed that other people saw during the crusade. But I remember the evangelist telling the story of 'little Jimmy Wiles'.

At one of his crusades in the USA he preached his usual or maybe I should say, *unusual* message because you didn't hear this kind of message every day. Jimmy Wiles, a young lad, was told that Oral Roberts was coming to town but Jimmy was a cripple and because, I believe, of polio, he wore leg braces and built-up shoes. On hearing that Oral Roberts was coming to town, Jimmy told his mother that he must go to hear him and get prayed for to heal his legs.

Jimmy instructed his mother to go and buy him 'normal' shoes ready for when God would heal him. His mother saw the boy's faith and duly complied. They attended the services of the

Faith - The Working Factors

crusade but night after night the prayer queues were full and he couldn't get near the preacher.

As Oral Roberts left the auditorium one evening, he walked along a lower corridor past a room where the door was open and passing, saw a little boy sat with his head in his hands looking downhearted. "What's the matter son", he asked the boy. "I'm supposed to get healed tonight", came the reply. "Well son, Oral Roberts is very tired and when he's tired sometimes his faith isn't so good", the evangelist replied "But I'm supposed to be healed tonight!" came the reply. "Son, I'm Oral Roberts", the evangelist said. "You are? Well I'm supposed to be healed tonight!" came the persistent claim. Oral Roberts told us that, 'By this time he had me', so I told him, "Well son, I tell you what I'll do. I'll lay my hand on you and pray but you'll have to do the believing!"

The evangelist saw nothing different after he had prayed and thought, 'Mmm, yes, that's what I thought'.

Faith - The Working Factors

They all left the auditorium and when Jimmy got home he again instructed his mother to go and get his new shoes. He put them on and told his mother, "You go and stand over there, one end of the room and I'll stand over here and I'll walk to you". As he began to walk, his legs suddenly got strong and he made it all the way across the room unaided.

When they arrived at the arena the next night, it broke up the meeting as the little boy walked in. When he went to school the next day it broke up the class.

I remember Oral Roberts declaring, "I've long since found out, that it's not how hard you pray or how loud you pray, you just have to believe". Many in that service got healed that day, I'm sure it was because they believed after hearing Jimmy Wiles' story.

JUST Believe! Let go of the doubt and fear and unbelief and trust God. Jesus said, "Have faith in God!" Let go of the, 'other' stuff and don't doubt. There are so many 'crazy' stories of God's healing

Faith - The Working Factors

power out there, crazy to us but normal to God and to those that just believe.

There will be more miracles and healings ahead, once you believe.

Chapter Thirteen
Belief is the key.

A miracle turns a non-believer into a believer. What we previously thought suddenly gets swept aside and a new concept arrives. We immediately conceive of a new thought, that what we all along didn't 'see' mentally, is now established in a moment, as new vision. The 'miracle' could be anything '**super**'-natural that has happened through faith. As I was talking to my daughter about this book, she gave me a word that I haven't yet used in regard to believing. She said, testimonies of what God has done gives us **expectation**. There's really no way to say that differently, we need a new expectation of being able to leave a bad situation and see a new way forward when there didn't seem to be one possible. What I like about people's stories of faith is that they convey a real life example of what actually took place against all odds and unbelief and it confounded the doubters and the sceptics. REAL EXPECTATION now exists where an empty mind was before, on the matter.

Faith - The Working Factors

When I was at Bible College, our Principal, Pastor Omri Bowen who had been a missionary in Nigeria told us of how he was invited to a village chief's house for dinner. "It was a great privilege", he said, so we duly attended. The food was served and the Pastor gave thanks to God for the food and it was all laid out before us, he said, a lovely spread.

The Pastor conveyed, "As we were eating and the longer we ate, the Chief began to look agitated, and it came to a point where he looked almost frightened. 'Is anything wrong?' I asked the Chief, to which he replied with alarm, 'We put enough poison in that food to kill an elephant, why do you not die?'"

Pastor Bowen said, 'Many were born again because of the miracle but *we* just believed as we gave thanks for the food'. We never know what harm satan has laid up for us but in God's hands, we are safe.

The secret is to surrender to God. Putting all of your life in His hands and just believing that from there on He will take care of things is what

Faith - The Working Factors

matters. Hand your life over to Him and relax… God has got your back now, in fact, He has all of you. ***Rest, be at peace in His care.***

Sometimes it's just that simple. Don't make it complicated, God is not complicated. ***Believe!***

I have often heard God's voice speak to me. After hearing the story of little Samuel in Sunday School and how God spoke to him in the night as he lay in his bed, I have often opened my ears to him and my heart to Him. As that young lad, I said simply to God in a reverent sort of voice, laying in bed in the quiet of my bedroom like Samuel, "Speak Lord for your servant hears you". I'm sure that is where my prophetic ministry began. I learnt to listen and then speak what God said. It changes people's lives.

Look at the passage from 1 Samuel 3: "Now the LORD came and stood and called as at other times, "Samuel! Samuel!" And Samuel answered, "Speak, for your servant hears. "Then the LORD said to Samuel: "Behold, I will do something in Israel at which both ears of everyone who hears it will tingle."

Faith - The Working Factors

Now you can have an ordinary life or you can have the type of life where people hearing God's voice will 'tingle' with life and truth. I know which I would prefer. My voice as a youngster never had much authority to it ***but I've seen people healed at the sound of what God said.*** <u>I've seen hundreds born again at the sound of *His* voice.</u> So many lives changed, because I took a little step as a lad and simply asked God to speak to me. I took the step to simply believe.

Seeing is believing?
Not always. There are tricksters, illusionists and the slight of hand of people around us who can dupe you into believing them but once God shows you a miracle in whatever form it comes, you simply believe. There's another point here too, Jesus said, "Blessed are those who have not seen and yet have believed". You can believe without having *had* to see it happen. Sometimes we are in situations where we can't see the possibility of something happening but we know just the same that God can do what we need done because He has that honest truth to what He says and we trust Him.

Faith - The Working Factors

The secret to believing is to hear what God says and *know* that He keeps His word. ***If He says, "I am the Lord that heals you", then He means just that!"***

I admit that the majority of people can't often stretch their thinking to see that an invisible God can so influence us that He can actually heal our physical bodies. There are two aspects to this from my own personal point of view. Firstly when I was young and suffering with Asthma, I was just 7 or 8 years old. I was not a philosopher or huge thinker at that age. So I simply believed that the God they talked of in Sunday School could help me breathe at night. I heard the words of the Bible, that 'those that call on the name of the Lord will be saved' from their problems. ***I believed that*** and my breathing came easier when I said the name of Jesus. It *actually* did. Later when I was 21 or so and in Bible College and was plagued with Asthma attacks at night and able to read maybe with more deliberateness, I heard the voice of God in scripture saying, "When you lie down, you will not be afraid, you shall lie down and your sleep will be sweet" (Proverbs 3:24). Well that did it, such a dynamic and timely statement from God

Faith - The Working Factors

set my belief system right and I lay down in earnest and SLEPT, no Asthma attack, just sleep, every night since then. *Belief works!* Don't try and tell me it doesn't, **what God says works,** end of story.

Let me explain something from the original greek text of scripture. There are two greek words Pisti and Pisteuo, one means belief, the other means faith. Now although the two words are very similar in meaning from the trust angle, they are different by the Bible definition of faith. **'Faith'** is *'the substance'* of what you hoped for. Both words may both be 'camped' around the same desire but one is the desire and the other, faith, is the actual evidence of what you wanted. It's the car stood in front of you that you actually wished for. Faith is the final product that was produced by your belief and hope. Ok, in a way, it may not be too important to describe all the details about the matter but sometimes we need to know these things to make our understanding more complete.

To see the faith part of what you desire is to see the thing you desired actually there in front of you. Faith is the *substance* of what you hope for. It's

Faith - The Working Factors

the *evidence* of the unseen belief, the hope you had. So by those statements, you can see that the important thing here is to have a *lively* hope and ***good, sound belief.***

Hearing about miracles and stories of miraculous healing is the way to activate our belief for many things. They take us closer to believing that, 'With God all things are possible', just as Jesus said. It brings ***expectation instead of despair***. I always tell people who are born again to tell their story of salvation and/or to give to people the account of where God did a miracle in their lives.

Faith is such an important thing as those who have seen God save their lives or heal their sickness will tell you. Faith is a force for good that is meant to enable us to manage our lives with dominion power.

I well remember hearing a story of the founder of the Apostolic Church in Wales, UK and His brother. The Apostle, Daniel Powell Williams and his brother and Prophet Jones Williams were out in the car one day when a horse and cart came out of a field right in front of their car. Unable to avoid it

Faith - The Working Factors

in time, the Apostle swiftly shouted a command to the angels, or rather to one particular angel. "Up Gabriel!" At that point the car lifted up in the air and flew over the top of the horse and cart, saving everyone involved.

Now whether you have heard of that before or not, you now know, if you believe it, that in such a situation, it is possible for it to happen.

Another Pastor in the Apostolic Church (a church that came out of the Welsh Revival of 1904), was told by God to go to Philadelphia in the USA to preach the gospel of Jesus. As Pastor John Pridie crossed the Atlantic in the plane, the pilot came on the plane's intercom. "Ladies and Gentlemen we are experiencing trouble with one of our engines, we have to reduce altitude". Some time later another warning ensued on the plane's intercom about yet another engine beginning to fail and people began to get panicked at the idea of maybe it crashing in the middle of the Atlantic.

At this point, to the sound of people shouting and some beginning to scream in fear, Pastor John stood up in the plane's aisle and addressed the

Faith - The Working Factors

passengers. "Listen to me. I'm a Christian Pastor and God has sent me to preach the gospel in Philadelphia. Now if I get there, you will all get there". From that point, he had their attention, so he preached the gospel to them and many got born again. Sometime after this, the pilot came on the intercom once more and made the announcement, "I would like to tell you that the problems are over and we have all engines healthy again."

God can do *anything* and *everything* you need done, as Job confessed. After his confession to God, "I know you can do everything", all his problems disappeared. All that He had lost, and that included all his possessions and land, were returned to him with double what he had before. Listen though to the scripture, Job 42:10
"And the LORD restored Job's losses when he prayed for his friends. Indeed the LORD gave Job twice as much as he had before".

Do you notice that along with Job's losses being restored, Job had prayed for his friends. Jesus said quite clearly, "Seek first God's kingdom and His right-ness and all the things the heathen seek after will be given you". Doing the right things brings

Faith - The Working Factors

God's blessing and faith is rewarded with many miraculous events.

This is a major principle, another ***faith factor*** if you like. If we agree with God on all matters, when we align ourselves with Him and His thoughts and ideas, we allow all that He is, to flow into our lives. So His bountifulness, His power, His goodness and 'all His benefits' download into our beings.

Take a look for a moment at Psalm 103. Take a slow walk through it and deliberate on the Psalm and see the gains as the Psalmist relays the benefits that God gives us:

Psalm 103:1-22 NKJV

Bless the LORD, O my soul; And all that is within me, bless His holy name! Bless the LORD, O my soul, **And forget not all His benefits:** *Who* **forgives** *all your iniquities,* ***Who*** **heals** *all your diseases,* ***Who*** **redeems** *your* **life** *from destruction,* ***Who*** **crowns** *you* *with loving-kindness and tender mercies,* ***Who*** **satisfies** *your mouth with good things,* **So that** *your youth is renewed* like the eagle's. **The LORD executes righteousness and justice for all who are**

Faith - The Working Factors

oppressed. He made known His ways to Moses, His acts to the children of Israel. ***The LORD is merciful and gracious,*** Slow to anger, and abounding in mercy. He will not always strive with us, Nor will He keep His anger forever. He has not dealt with us according to our sins, Nor punished us according to our iniquities. For as the heavens are high above the earth, So great is His mercy toward those who fear Him; ***As far as the east is from the west, So far has He removed our transgressions from us.*** As a father pities his children, ***So the LORD pities those who fear Him.*** For He knows our frame; He remembers that we are dust. As for man, his days are like grass; As a flower of the field, so he flourishes. For the wind passes over it, and it is gone, And its place remembers it no more. ***But the mercy of the LORD is from everlasting to everlasting On those who fear Him,* And His righteousness to children's children,** To such as keep His covenant, And to those who remember His commandments to do them. The LORD has established His throne in heaven, And His kingdom rules over all. Bless the LORD, you His angels, Who excel in strength, who do His word, Heeding the voice of His word. Bless the LORD,

Faith - The Working Factors

all you His hosts, You ministers of His, who do His pleasure. Bless the LORD, all His works, in all places of His dominion. **Bless the LORD, O my soul!**

There are many Psalms like this. Psalm 91 is another and Psalm 23 too, they all enumerate the good things that God gives us. Falling into line with His ways has *such* benefits.

When we concur with the Holy Spirit within us, we can also pass on the *goodness,* the *benefits* of God to others. Jesus says about believers, 'they shall lay hands on the sick and they shall recover'…. etc., so agreeing with His ways allows the Holy Spirit within us to partner with us to bless others.

Chapter Fourteen
Partnering with God

The 'Alliance' we get from Salvation is the alliance of our lives. There is no greater partnership anywhere that gives people such a huge benefit as we read in Psalm 103 etc. Whereas we would sometimes fail and not have a hope of recovery, the joint between us and God is paramount to help us recover. God always intended to be by our side from the beginning as a partner to us, in friendship and fellowship. But it was more than that also, we are His family, His children, His joint-heirs and closest relations. We were so close to Him we were created bone of His bone, flesh of His flesh and Spirit of His Spirit.

Ok that closeness was spoilt when Adam rebelled against Him but the salvation that He provided was designed to bring back the family ties and restore our one-ness with Him. We have never known full one-ness with God, we were brought up in sin and shaped by iniquity, so far away from our Father. But the re-unity of being born again is what we all need. Distance from God is not good. Division from Father is making us lose not only our benefits

Faith - The Working Factors

but is making us lose the closeness of His Love and comforting presence. ***And this is a factor of faith too***. ' Faith works by love', scripture says. So our ability to do things that are miraculous, both for ourselves and for others is very important. The world needs to know about our loving Father and we need to see more and more the intimacy that is available with such a person as our great Almighty God, the lover of our souls.

God is love. We must dwell in love and as Jesus said, "Abide in my love". Jesus prayed that we should be one, that as the Father Abides in Him so we need to abide in the Father and the Father in us. It's a powerful notion that Jesus introduces us to and prays for us to have. "That they may be one as we are one". Just read …. John 17:21-24 NKJV (By the way if you don't have the Bible in various new versions, they are all on line, just go to www.bible.com and get a free Bible for your phone or ipad or PC)

"…That they all may be one, as You, Father, are in Me, and I in You; that they also may be one in Us, that the world may believe that You sent Me. [22] And the glory which You gave Me I have given them, that they may be one just as We are one:

Faith - The Working Factors

[23] I in them, and You in Me; that they may be made perfect in one, and that the world may know that You have sent Me, and have loved them as You have loved Me. [24] "Father, I desire that they also whom You gave Me may be with Me where I am, that they may behold My glory which You have given Me; for You loved Me before the foundation of the world."

God wants us back. He wants us one with Him, so close that ***His*** strength is ***our*** strength, His power is our power, His thoughts are our thoughts, that we think like He thinks, His mind is our mind. Scripture talks about 'the renewing of our minds' and us 'Having the mind of Christ'. All those weak ideas and lack of initiatives ***gone*** and good thinking, strong thinking, ours again. **Partnership.**

One-ness with the Father and creator of our beings brings such rewards. We were meant to partner with our creator, to be associated with Him in love and joy, to know His peaceful ways every day and enjoy His pleasant ways and His wisdom. Proverbs says about His Wisdom, "All her ways are pleasantness and all her paths are peace".

Faith - The Working Factors

The association with the Almighty is embracing and close. When we have His company, His Spirit in us, we lack for nothing. The Holy Spirit, the Comforter, the Helper, the Teacher of all things is here to make our lives great again. Alienation from God has made us poor but He wants us rich in every way. Look at the old testament's words, "Rise up and shout, you inhabitant of Zion for great is the Holy one of Israel in the midst of you!" That says it all. As God's children with His presence in the middle of us, we learn to rise and be successful in all that we do. The initiative to rise is resident within us from the point of being born again - His Spirit is *life.*

God said regarding Adam, "It is not good for man to be alone", so He made Eve as a partner for him. Company and partnership is good when it's a proper relationship. Today in the world we see very little of good relationships with divorce and marriage break-ups on the increase, with no long term love happening. But God says, "I have loved you with an everlasting love". Much satisfaction is lost in this world because there are so many things that let us down, especially in terms of relationships with people. But the fellowship we

Faith - The Working Factors

should have had from the beginning should be strong and good with love as the basis unhindered by offence and upset. God IS love and His world, Heaven, is a pure love environment. We have always known a society which has disturbed and hurtful relationships but that was never instituted by God, this was satan's work having caused rebellion between people. We have to imagine the world to come where love rules everywhere. In the 'Millenium' period a new order will exist when Christ will rule in love and during this period we will see big changes to the earth. 'The lion will lie down with the lamb and a crawling baby will put its hand into the snakes nest and not be bitten. In the vegetation world we will see differences too, where instead the thorn bushes will come up myrtle trees and so on. The harm throughout society will be gone. God's redemption will be an all-encompassing one, so that His nature will be seen throughout and there will be *peace*.

And this is a factor in the faith narrative too. Faith is an attribute that fits in with all of God's world and it works to redress the faults and failings in the world. If faith comes from hearing what God says and we get our faith that way, then faith

Faith - The Working Factors

has God's repairing, replenishing and healing character running through it. We need to see this point because then we will see that faith has a repairing and saving nature to it, as does all of God's character. ***There is a pattern here.*** It is that God is so evidently all love. People fail to see that God is not malicious in any way. Even when God destroys, He does it to destroy things that harm or prey on people. Again, it is not easy to see from our sinful angle that God only destroys evil, He is at all times only loving. Take great note of the fact of why He does things the way He does, it is because He is love. To appreciate who God is in His character is so important, especially as we are made in His image and likeness. God is our greatest example if we fully understand Him.

Being a loving God means that He has no fear. Indeed, why should He fear? There is nothing or anyone that can overthrow Him or put Him under any pressure. He is Almighty. But being love, there is no animosity in Him. There is no offence in Him, neither does He take offence. Indeed, the way He deals with our offences is to sacrifice Himself to protect us and save us. Jesus said, "No man takes my life from me (there's His

Faith - The Working Factors

omnipotence and strength), I lay it down of myself." He gave His life for us to live, **that's love!** But *His* love is the greatest we have ever seen. He put down fear and disregarded it in order to make us free and love us by going to the cross.

To rise from death, He had nothing to hold Him there. There was no bondage to fear, He stood up fear and hell and pain and torment and went to the cross suffering the agony of it, *to set us free* from fear and death and hell.

Why am I saying this is in this book about Faith? It's because the strength of our Faith is based on His Faith, the strength of it and we have His of type of faith, His measure of faith. Scripture says that 'To each is given the measure of faith'. Romans 12:3 KJV.

We are given **the** measure of faith. Another scripture says that we have the faith **of** Christ Galatians 2:16." A man is not justified by the works of the law, but by the faith of Jesus Christ; we have believed in Jesus Christ, that we might be justified *by* the faith of Christ."

Faith - The Working Factors

It's all about His faith and us getting our faith like His faith, we are justified in our beliefs by His faith. I always say that when He created us and when we are 'Born-again' he made us just like Himself. We got two arms and 2 legs and all the other parts that God has. He didn't leave out faith, we got faith like Him too. It's part of the partnering with Him. He was raised from death triumphing over it entirely *so that* we can have power over it too. He did it **for us**. Look at Isaiah 53....' He was wounded *for* our transgressions, bruised *for* our iniquities, He was chastised *for* our peace and *by* His stripes *we are healed*'. What a partnership! He gave us a partnership with Himself and we never did anything to be deserving of it.

He just says, 'Go into all the world and preach the gospel to every creature….. baptise them and heal them, cast out their demons and set them free with faith and power'….. and *'lo I am with you always,* even unto the end of the world'. What a partnership.

Chapter Fifteen
Reign – Faith ruling.

'***Don't let*** your heart be troubled'. ***Neither let it be*** afraid. John 14: 1. **You are to reign.**

Of all the things we need to reign over and govern, *fear* is one of the most beneficial to rule over and *get rid of*. We've spoken of fear and faith, that fear rules us very often where faith should be ruling. ***We can't have both faith and fear***. One has to go. Fear has no useful function to us and we need to remember that all our assets from God are good and not use-less.

But look at what Jesus says in John 14. He says quite clearly, "Don't let you hear heart be troubled or afraid. I always thought, for some reason, that Jesus was referring to the future when we go to heaven because He is referring to His Father's house. In fact, He has already gone to prepare a place for us and this place is where He now reigns and rules from. Jesus is saying that we are to rule over fear and trouble ***now***. We are to reign from the perspective of the place He has prepared for us.

Faith - The Working Factors

It is quite clear, "***Let not*** your heart be troubled!" That's NOW. Rule now. "Neither let it be afraid!" And that's NOW as well. That's the faith way. Our wrong thinking and our laziness often puts off some of our faith thinking because we have been so long without any good ideas that we don't realise that we should be on top of things all the time.

God wants a *victorious* life for us. A life of dominion as He meant for Adam. '*Your heart not being troubled', is just that.* God's household is a house of normal dominion and rule without any care or bother.

Jesus always had a place for us. He has a mansion for us. See now, we need to appreciate the name 'mansion'. We don't have a mediocre future, we have a future with a mansion and the 'normal' is mansion life.

Salvation is a much bigger, much more all-embracing subject than we usually understand. God doesn't do things by halves. His salvation as the hymn-writer says is a FULL salvation.

Faith - The Working Factors

Everything that Adam was given for a full and complete life, is ours in salvation.

So when Jesus says, 'Don't let your heart be troubled' He is referring to the mode of life you should expect. Not being afraid is part of that same creation. Life means LIFE. A good life is not being afraid and not being curtailed in how you live. No wonder Paul says to the Galatian people, "Stand fast in the liberty wherewith Christ has made you free and don't be entangled again with the yoke of bondage". You were called to be *free*.

Jesus said, "In my Father's house are many mansions. I go to prepare a place for you *so that* where I am, you shall be also". That place of being where Jesus is, denotes once again our *position* in faith. In Ephesians chapter 1, we read of our understanding being enlightened so that we may see our position in Christ. From verse 15 onwards we see the hope of our calling and our inheritance as children of God. Note that from there to the end of the chapter there are no full stops, only commas in the punctuation. We start off being shown who we are and end up in the

Faith - The Working Factors

throne where Jesus is. It was something I didn't realise until it was pointed out to me.

See now, we can miss huge detail if we are not careful but the detail is so important. Paul speaks of our eyes being opened to who we are and what our inheritance is and then what is the exceeding greatness of God's power which is given to us. The power he refers to is that same resurrection-power that raised Jesus from the dead and then seated Him in heavenly places far above all other beings, is where we are heading. Now that's not readily visible as a route for us but that's what scripture says and is why Paul is praying that we get our eyes opened and then see the hope of God's calling to us.

We need to be unafraid and not troubled in our hearts and the reassurances of who we are, are there to be seen in the Bible. We just need to feed our belief system and our faith with them.

The words of God, if we ***believe*** them, will promote us and cause us to rise to where God wants us. When I was suffering with chronic Asthma at night and couldn't sleep, I went to God

Faith - The Working Factors

and demanded that something was done. I said, "You have got to tell me something that will change this situation!". God immediately gave me a scripture in Proverbs 3:24 NKJV. It read: "When you lie down, you will not be afraid; Yes, you will lie down and your sleep will be sweet." *That was my mandate to sleep at night.* I went to bed that night and read what God had said. I then said to Him,...."*You said it, I believe it, now I'm going to sleep!"* I slept all night and every night after that. No Asthma attack ever stopped me sleeping again.

Following and believing Jesus' words is the enablement to *do* what His words *say*.

You can rule your situations, if you wait on God and hear what He says. God's voice is the guide to success. *His words are the ruling factor* and *carry* His authority. It was His words that brought the world into being and kicked off the creation of life.... "Let there be light". I like the way Genesis 1 explains how God set about making all things. We are told firstly that 'In the beginning, God created the heavens and the earth and then He gets down to the creative detail of the earth and its

138

Faith - The Working Factors

readiness for civilisation. So just watch what God does first. His Spirit hovers over the waters. It's as though He is microscopically viewing the materials He has made available. Then He speaks to begin the process of life. "Let there be light". Notice that God doesn't deal in darkness, His ways are truth and intellectually profound. Light is the ingredient to bring life and warmth to plants and cause growth. Light is movement and energy. Note that all of God's power is lively and creative and we need just that light, that truth in our faith because our faith will need to create answers to problems and bring life to areas of death or difficulty.

In Hebrews 11, I would like you to see just how many different ways God's people worked faith wonders by using their faith. Look at the catalogue of faith people listed there and what they did with their faith:

Abel, Enoch, Noah, Abraham, Sarah, Isaac, Jacob, Joseph, Moses, Rahab, Gideon, Barak, Samson, Jephthah, David, Samuel and the prophets...., and look what they did, Hebrews 11:11,13,33-40 NKJV

Faith - The Working Factors

By faith Sarah herself also received strength to conceive seed, and *she bore a child when she was past the age,* because she judged Him (God) faithful who had promised. [13] These all died in faith, not having received the promises, but having seen them afar off were assured of them, embraced them and confessed that they were strangers and pilgrims on the earth. [33] *who through faith subdued kingdoms, worked righteousness,* obtained promises, *stopped the mouths of lions,* [34] *quenched the violence of fire, escaped the edge of the sword,* out of weakness *were made strong, became valiant in battle,* [35] *Others were tortured, not accepting deliverance,* that they might obtain a better resurrection. [36] *Still others had trials of mockings and scourgings,* yes, *and of chains and imprisonment.* [37] *They were stoned, they were sawn in two, were tempted, were slain with the sword.* They wandered about in sheepskins and goatskins, *being destitute, afflicted, tormented-* [38] of whom the world was not worthy. *They wandered in deserts and mountains, in dens and caves of the earth.* [39] And all these, having obtained a good testimony through faith, did not receive the promise, [40]

Faith - The Working Factors

God having provided something better for us, that they should not be made perfect apart from us."

One of the messages, as I have previously said, I have preached widespread in Africa and other places is that, '**With God all things are possible**' and I like to tell of many, many testimonies showing what faith can do. There is nothing like hearing what God has done to create faith and belief in the hearts of people. *This is how we learn to reign over evil in this world* and **Faith is key.**

Chapter Sixteen
The Surrender Factor

Faith is a winning substance, an evidence of internal strength and might put there by God's Spirit when we got born again. We can surrender to our problems and to those forces that try and subject us or we can surrender our lives to a mightier power whose name is Almighty God.

The onslaught to try and make us surrender may come from satan or from our old flesh and memories, or even from our best friends and relatives in this world. Remember in the book of Job where even his wife says to him in the middle of his conflict, "Why don't you just curse God and die?"

Now that's hard but see now, we are under no compunction to give in and surrender to death and wrong. With God in us ('In the midst of us') we don't have to surrender. When I was a young man, just newly married about a year, everything was going fine for me. I had a lovely new wife and we had found out that we had a baby on the way in about 6 months time. I was working all hours to

Faith - The Working Factors

get our house ready for sale to move and busy in church on the weekend. Suddenly I started getting pains in the chest. The pains would hit me hard and it frightened me. I couldn't tell Helen my wife. We were both so happy, how could I ruin it all with such an announcement? And then there was my fear, I was afraid to go to the doctor in case he gave me some horrible diagnosis. I know that sounds silly but fear backs you into a corner and all sorts of bad things go through your mind.

I remember locking myself in the bathroom. I needed a quiet place where I could try and relax, somewhere I could pour my heart and feelings out to God and reach out to Him for help.

At that point satan said to me, "You'll never see your child born". It's awful to be kicked so hard when you are already frightened and feeling so alone against a backdrop of the best time of your life. What a comedown from the highest heights to the lowest depths.

But in that bathroom that day, I learned to surrender myself. Was it to satan? No definitely

Faith - The Working Factors

not. Did David surrender to Goliath? No. So neither was I about to surrender to satan or fear.

As I sat there on the lid of the toilet, I sobbed to the Lord Jesus. Now and again the pain would hit my chest and I would fear and almost await the end. It would come randomly like a bolt of lightning in my chest.

Then, as I surrendered my feelings to God, inspiration came in a very odd way. I said "OK Lord, if you want to take me home, just do it, don't mess me about though, I don't believe in having sickness!" It was my declaration of faith and trust and everything else my soul could muster to empty myself of me and my ideas and put my reliance, in the worst of situations, into the hands of the Almighty.

I sat there, waiting for God to take me home. I waited and waited. Was He not going to answer me? Is He being cruel? NO, I reasoned, God wasn't cruel, He was kind. So what *was* going on, apart from seemingly nothing? I waited and waited. Then Helen called me from downstairs. "I'm in the bathroom!" I replied. And after as long a wait as I could sustain, trying to grip the

Faith - The Working Factors

situation with my hopes and beliefs, I went downstairs. I put on a brave face and kept the truth from her. I couldn't bring myself to tell her. I kept this horrible secret inside me, just telling only God.

For weeks the pains kept coming randomly. They would come when I was in the electronics workshop at work or when I was in the garden. I prayed for healing. God had already taken away asthma that I suffered with at night, so I prayed for health.

After a while, nothing happened, I didn't get called home to Heaven, so then another thought came to me, 'Maybe God is going to heal me'.

As the months went by, the pains grew less and my confidence began to grow. The anxiety diminished to a point where after about 6 months, I was beginning to feel normal. But it was a tense time and one where I learned to fully trust God and surrender all to Him.

There are two things we can do. Surrender to fear or to satan and evil or surrender to a mightier

Faith - The Working Factors

power, tp surrender to the Almighty God, to the Saviour, to Jesus. It was what I learned to do over that traumatic period and God delivered me out of it.

I saw my son born and we started living better and better, *with some trials* but now with someone at my back, looking after me and I began to grow more as a believer. Faith was doing its work in me.

It often doesn't occur to us that there is another type of surrender. We have only one concept usually of it. But we can learn to give in to a better power, a more intelligent power that can and will help us out when we need help. He is our creator, the one who loves us, the one who *surrendered* Himself to go to the cross, to save us **when** we needed saving, like in that awful moment in the bathroom.

It was a stroke of genius on God's part, to prompt me to ask Him to take me home if He wanted to. In so doing I took satan out of the equation and only relied on God. **I Surrendered**. It was surrender in a way that I would never have thought

Faith - The Working Factors

of but it was a proper and right surrender. haven't looked back on that day when God taught me to trust Him.

I often say to people, 'when you find a new way to surrender to God or find something in your life you haven't surrendered to God yet, ***Just do it, full and wholeheartedly***. It brings such a relief and takes the tension away to know that yet another part of you is now in God's safe hands.

We have talked of our safety in this book, of faith taking us out of situations that were dangerous for us. We have talked of many factors, of many people who survived because they called on God with faith, believing in Him. But really, it's because they gave their lives over to the Almighty, greatest power of all, rather than give in to wrong and to weakness.

You see, at the end of the day, we don't have to die and our situations don't have to die. We can always call on God and surrender ourselves to Him. Our circumstances don't have to have death implanted within them, we can have good lives with good outcomes but sometimes we need to

Faith - The Working Factors

relinquish bad thinking and poor living habits and surrender to better ways and more prosperous ideas, that only God has.

Did you think that we will only have an easy life?

Now this book is about faith and the working factors of faith. Faith works. It does what scripture says it will do. Often though there are things that need wheedling out of our lives, like fear and we get power over them by simply standing firm and trusting God when hard moments come along. Jesus said to Simon Peter in Luke 22, 31... "Simon, Simon! Indeed, Satan has asked for you, that he may sift you as wheat. [32] But I have prayed for you, that your faith should not fail; and when you have returned to Me, strengthen your brethren."

We *will* get trials, it's the way the problem areas of our lives are sifted outt. ***What you need to remember firmly is that Jesus has prayed for us*** and is sat talking to the Father in Heaven about our trials. Jesus said to Simon Peter, "I have prayed for you, ***that your faith should* not fail**; and **when**

Faith - The Working Factors

you have returned to Me, *strengthen your brethren."*

Notice that Jesus says, "WHEN", not IF but when. We need to read all of scripture meaningfully and see what it *actually* says, not what our fear makes us think that it says. Sometimes problems in life will call on us to make decisions about where we are in life and what we believe and where our faith can lead us. In those moments we need to look to someone who can help us and not to one who can destroy us. *Surrender.* Be happy to do it knowing that it leads to a good conclusion. **Trust God.**

Chapter Seventeen
The Sustenance Factor

Can my faith sustain me always? - The BIG question. Well let's just look at the question. Is it *my* faith…… Did I manufacture it? NO. It was it faith given me by God? Scripture says quite clearly as we've already quoted in this book, 'To each is *given*, the measure of faith'. So if it were just *your* faith, it might fail. If I consider the 'faith' I had before I got born again, I would fail with *that* faith. It was what I was born with, and I was 'born in sin and shaped by iniquity' so my faith was rotten at the core. But see now, I got born again, I asked God to forgive me for my sin and asked Him into my life and to teach me His ways and give me *His* faith. ***So why should my <u>new</u> faith not sustain me?*** It's *my* faith by choice of my free will ***but it came as a gift from God***, so why should it not *always* sustain me?

I've worded that very carefully because we need to understand the 'mechanics' of how we got our new faith. 1. God presented salvation to us, 2. We accepted it with our free will (God won't have it any other way) and 3. I received a brand new faith

150

Faith - The Working Factors

enlivened and made alive by His Spirit. So *my* faith is really ***His faith made alive in me***. That's very important. Scripture says, "We have the faith of Christ". Stop for a moment, look at that scripture. Do you realise *what* Jesus did with His faith? Look at all the miracles. He stopped the storm on the lake, He raised the dead, He healed the lepers, the blind, the paralysed, the lame, the fevered.... John says that if all the things Jesus did with His faith were recorded, we couldn't write them all down.

Let's go back a step and see what happened after Jesus died on the cross. He gave up His Spirit into God's - His Father's hands. Taking all our sins, He descended into hell and death and took the keys of death and hell and He now has them on His person. Jesus was then raised from death by the Spirit of God and He now lives forever having authority in His whole being over all things. His faith declared, 'All power is given to me in Heaven and in earth'. Then He said to the disciples, '***Therefore*** go teach all nations baptising them in the name of the Father, the Son and the Holy Spirit.' ... 'Cast out demons, raise the dead,

Faith - The Working Factors

cleanse the lepers, lay hands on the sick and they shall recover'. 'See the faith in action?

Whatever we are told to do by God, the enablement of the words of God is there to sustain the work He asks us to do. We may *feel* we don't have the ability or we cannot sustain that idea but God says for us to do it.

Faith is not a weak thing. It wasn't weakness that raised Jesus from the dead, it was the power of God's Spirit. We saw on the day of Pentecost dramatic changes in the disciples after they were all filled with the Holy Spirit. Timid, fearful Peter now stands up and preaches a bold sermon and then he and John heal a crippled beggar at the gate of Jerusalem. "We don't have silver and gold to give you **but such as we do have, we give you, *get up and walk"***, they said and the man jumped and leaped and praised God immediately.

Faith will not only sustain you but it sustains the message you now have for the world. We need to consider seriously the sustenance factor of faith.

Faith - The Working Factors

God gives us hope in our spirit to believe ***and do*** things that we couldn't sustain before. We couldn't get our heads around believing for these things before but the lively hope He gives us, not only shows us what is possible but enlivens, 'quickens', our faith to do what He says we can do.

Sustained. - Kept living when all else says we can't survive. If God can raise the dead where even bodies are deceased and void, empty of all life, then He can do anything we need done.

Remember, "With God all things are possible" but then Jesus says, "If **you** believe, ***all things are possible!"***

Our minds might not yet sustain that thought but if we surrender our thoughts to God, He can enliven our thinking with His initiatives.

I remember my wife Helen saying to me one day when she had a particular need that was really bothering her, "God says you have to pray for me". I recall not being able to sustain that thought because I didn't know *what* to pray for, her problem was a complex issue she had in her mind

Faith - The Working Factors

and I hadn't a clue of where to start. I went before God about it and God spoke to me. He said "Anoint her with oil and pray". "But Lord", I said, "I don't know *what* to pray". Then God spoke to me again and said, "Put oil on your own head *first* and *then* pray" (oil is the symbol of God's Spirit, the one who raised Jesus from the dead). Immediately my mind came alive and I heard my mind say, *'That would work'*. So I anointed myself, then Helen and I started to pray. My mind went from empty to full in moments and what I prayed caused a reaction immediately and she retched and heaved and the problem was GONE. "I'm free, it's gone" was her response.

God is the sustenance you need to do whatever your faith needs done. He is the food our soul needs to get the job done. If you need a new initiative or idea, a notion to change your thinking, then He is the one you need.

One of the 'fruits' of God's Spirit listed in Galatians chapter 5 is 'Longsuffering', the ability to suffer long or 'endure'. We so often need to keep going when our patience is being stretched to breaking point but God's strength, which never

Faith - The Working Factors

gives out, is there for us. His Spirit is life everlasting. God is enduring in every way.

Look at the 3 Hebrew lads in the old testament. They are put in a furnace for not bowing down to a foreign idol god. As they were thrown into the furnace, the men who put them in there were killed by the heat. But when people looked in, they saw a fourth person standing with them. Whereas no ordinary person could endure that furnace, this 'other' one could withstand anything *and* protect those with Him. God stands with you, not only in principle but in reality. As you believe His words, His words protect you because they have His Spirit behind them. When the three lads came out of the furnace, they didn't even have the smell of smoke on them. ***Sustained!***

Faith *comes* from hearing God's word's. We hear the sense of what He says and that 'sensible' expression sustains us as we adhere to it. The word of God endures forever. 1 Peter 1:25. God is an everlasting, eternal God. His words endure just like He does. So when we believe His words, they sustain us *forever*.

Faith - The Working Factors

We need to follow through the notions that are found in the Bible. They don't just last for a moment, they progress and produce far more truth as we follow them.

Chapter Eighteen
Faith Tested Out

We often dodge the thought that our faith needs testing. We may have a weakness of some kind in our belief system or we don't seem to have hope for some things. Often we come across problems where we can't seem to find the belief to get over some hurdles, whether it's a certain type of sickness or maybe we just can't appear to speak up in some situations. On occasions where certain people are around us, we don't seem to be able to speak boldly about our faith, we seem to clam up.

Many of the great people of faith were tested, to see where they were in relation to what they believed:- Abraham, Job, Stephen, Peter, etc. It was not a sentence to hardship when they were tested by God, it's often to just help us root out the weaknesses and wrong understanding that we have, to get rid of the false doctrines about faith that prevent us operating in full strength faith. When God tests us it's always to get something better going on in us than what we had before, to bring a new measure of life to work in us.

Faith - The Working Factors

Take Abraham for example. God asks him to do a very hard thing, "Take your son, Isaac and sacrifice him to me". Now there are a number of things going on with this arduous test. Firstly, many of the people around that area where Abraham lived were sacrificing their children to their gods. Secondly, where did Abraham's allegiance lay, with the people around him or did he believe their practices were wrong? Thirdly, what did Abraham believe about *his* God? Was his God like the other gods? And of course above all, would Abraham *do* what God told him even though he didn't think his God would ask him to do such a thing?

Do you see the trial? It's *many* tests in one. What does Abraham believe about God and would he do what his God asked him to do despite all the emotions and the wrongness of it. And then Abraham had the promise that in his seed all the nations of the earth would be blessed. How could that be if his son was sacrificed? Where would the future be then?

Abraham of course follows God's request out of what seems to be blind faith because God said to

Faith - The Working Factors

do it. He would have gone through with the deed and done what God had asked of him. Isaac was trussed and bound on the altar, the fire was ready to consume the sacrifice….. The knife was poised in the air ready to strike….. Then God stopped the trial. He knew what He wanted to know about Abraham and the moment he was told to stop and do no harm to the boy, another was made available to take Isaac's place. God provided a ram to provide His own sacrifice to take Isaac's place. The lesson is that if we do what God tells us, we don't have to suffer, God will take care of the issue.

It's sometimes very important that God proves us to see what we believe and whether we will do as He asks and when He does, we get the blessing of it.

I was once away on a training course in the Midlands with British Telecom. I was resident there for the duration of the course situated in the college's accommodation. I needed fellowship and somewhere to get alone with God as well where I could talk to him with no interruption. One evening I decided to get in the car and just

Faith - The Working Factors

drive around until I found a quiet spot to pray and just let God communicate with me.

It was a dark autumn night and it was hard to find the right location in the unlit lanes of the Stafford countryside. The evening was very dark. And as I drove, God spoke to me. "I want you to bow the knee to me". *I was delighted*. God had asked me to do something for Him and this I could do and I was happy to comply. I stopped the car in this dark country lane and began to think about where I could kneel down. I couldn't kneel in the driving position, there was no room, so I wondered about the back of the car. There was no room there either. I would have to get out of the car and kneel in the road. Then the problems started; satan and my flesh began putting up the excuses.

What if a car comes around the corner? There were no lights on the road. I could be killed. Then there was the possible humiliation of being seen kneeling, praying in front of my car on a dark road…, if anyone came… etc… etc, the excuses kept coming. But listen, God asked me to do it so I was going to do what He asked whatever happened. I *wanted* to do something for Him and

Faith - The Working Factors

so I got out of the car. I made my way around to the front of the car and calmly knelt in honour of my God and I determined not to rush it but stayed there and poured out my heart. "I am pleased to do this Father, you are my God and I bow my knees before you….." When I had said all I wanted to say I got up and went back to the car. As I opened the door and got into the driving seat my spirit got the understanding that I had just made everything within me, righteous or unrighteous bow the knee to the Almighty God. *I got such a joy out of that,* especially making all the wrong stuff in me bow down and worship God. *It was a turning point in my life.* I had physically brought everything into subjection to God, my Saviour. You should try it sometime, it's amazing.

Take a look for a moment then at Job's life. At the beginning of the book of Job he was susceptible to so many things that Satan could pin on him. He basically did his sacrificing out of fear and not out of right conviction. *We* can do that. We can simply do the right things because we fear God will do something bad to us, which is a totally wrong concept of who God is. What we need is a proper understanding of Him, that He is a God of

Faith - The Working Factors

love, not a God who is out to get us and harm us. "If God be for us who, can be against us?" (Romans 8) Does that ring a bell? God is love. For God SO loved the world, that He gave his only son that whoever believes on Him ***will not*** perish but ***have*** everlasting life. God did not send his son into the world to condemn the world but that the world through Him might be SAVED. Ring any bells?

For some reason we don't always think this way. The reason…. Is that we were brought up *in* sin and *by* sin and shaped in our thinking by iniquity.

Job went through a process that God instituted and called satan's attention to. He said to satan, "Have you considered my servant Job, that there are none as righteous as him?" I can imagine satan saying, 'Just take your hedge of protection from around him and we'll see what kind of guy Job is'. What we don't realise is that Job *was* a good guy. He just had some fear problems that he needed to get rid of so that his faith could come to the fore.

God has ways to deal with our fear if we will trust Him and the result of losing that fear is to make

Faith - The Working Factors

our faith free to operate. So God takes Job on a journey. All the things that worry him most happen to him when satan gets his hands on Job. Then God tells satan, "But don't touch his life!" God is not out to destroy us or our righteous children or relatives. But He *is* out to destroy our fears and get us rid of them.

Throughout a great part of Job's life he suffers because of his fear. He gets fear related plagues, boils etc. He loses his unrighteousness land and possessions. Even Job's wife tells him to curse God and die and to put himself out of his misery. ***But Job hangs in there.*** The faith he has in the Almighty is made clearer to him and he gains understanding even though his friends try to argue this and that with him.

Sometimes we need to examine closely exactly what we believe to see if it's <u>righteous</u> or <u>just religious.</u> If we don't test what we believe in this world of deceit and trickery we will be left with impure areas in our lives and that will cost us dearly. In terms of faith, we will lose strength where we need our faith to work and we need it to work well. When trials come we need straight, no

163

Faith - The Working Factors

nonsense faith, we don't need to be scrambling around wishing we knew how to pray or what words we needed to pray or what we should believe in a given situation. God always meant us to know the truth, the whole truth and nothing but the truth, so the **entire** truth would set us fully free. God wants us **FULLY FREE.**

By the end of God's dealing with Job, after all Job's trials, Job makes a very great statement to God that is very revealing of what he now believes, *"I know that you can do everything!"*
He now KNOWS that God can do everything he needs. There is NOTHING outside of his belief system that God can't do for him. After all of satan's messing and interfering with his life, Job knows his God's ability and his faith in that ability to help him is complete. Watch the outcome ….

Immediately Job confesses that to God, all his troubles disappear.

We need to start making proper statements of faith *based on what we believe and know about the Almighty*. Job gets back all his land and possessions and his fortune doubles. See now,

Faith - The Working Factors

that's faith working properly. There's no lack in Job's life now, there's only prosperity.

If we know and trust God, then why do we fear? God is only going to do us good. So why preach any other message other than 'GOD IS GOOD', - <u>all the time God is good.</u> There's no time when He's not good. We need to shed the fears and lack of trust in Him and make the statement like Job, "I know you can do everything, not just anything I need done but EVERYTHING I NEED DONE.

We need to get satan's stuff out of our lives, we need to be rid of his meddling and interfering ways. We need to ***stop*** being scared of Satan and we need to insist on our righteousness being the foremost authority and ***put down*** the strongholds of satan. <u>We are not empty of goodness,</u> we have God's goodness. We are not void of right-ness, ***we are right because God makes us right in salvation.***

If a trial or two sorts out the wrong bits in our lives we should welcome a trial or two. We will be stronger for having to trust God when everything seems to be going wrong. It's how we prove that

Faith - The Working Factors

God is for us and not against us. We get to prove what we already knew of Him in our hearts.

1 Peter 1:7... The trial of your faith, being much more precious than of gold that perishes, though it be tried with fire, might be found unto praise and honour and glory at the appearing of Jesus Christ:

We are more than conquerors through Him who loves us. We may go through trials but God only sends us *through* problems to *get better results out of our faith*. **He knows what we are capable of**, He's the one who re-birthed us and got us born-again.

Will He test us beyond what we can bear? NO.
Will He in any way risk us? NO.
Will He do anything that will cause us unnecessary worry? NO.
God only has our interests in mind.
Is He working to make us bigger than we were? YES. He is always working with us, 'To will and to do of His good pleasure'. His will for us is to improve our situation in **all** ways. Our problem is in realising that God is at work to improve us in every way.

Faith - The Working Factors

Often children do not like being told to 'grow up' and behave rightly and stop being childish. But let's be honest, often we need to be told those things. Sometimes we *are* being childish, sometimes we *do* need to grow up and be adult in our actions, sometimes we *need* to behave properly and in an adult manner. Often parents have to say these things. Is God any different? No. He wants us mature and sensible in every way and He wants us to grow and be responsible for our lives. We sometimes set our children targets to make them realise they need to mature and be better.

We shouldn't 'despise the chastening of the Lord' as the Bible tells us. We should in fact be pleased that God is wanting to mature us and make us stronger and better.

We need to be tested sometimes, we need to be checked out and when we are, we should rejoice when we pass the tests and become stronger for it. Our faith should be tested and it should grow as God wants it to. Testing is often a factor of our faith and to see that our faith works is a great bonus to our confidence.

Chapter Nineteen
Faith – Not being seduced away

Faith is our heritage from God. We have this great gift, backed up by His Spirit that can do anything, if we believe what God says.

But there are forces that would often try and seduce us away from either using our faith or thinking in faith terms.

We have dealt with doubt, - double mindedness, in this book. We have alluded to many of the things that take from us our belief and hope but there are many things that subtly and cleverly on satan's part that try and deceive us. I often look at some of the statements we make in our churches, we have already touched on many of them, such as 'I don't know if it is God's will to heal me'.

We were singing a worship song in church one day and we were all fairly lost in the act of just loving God for what He had done for us. The song spoke of our desires to love God, deeply and fully and we sang, "And I long to worship you", which seemed so wonderful but in the middle of that I heard a

Faith - The Working Factors

voice deep in my soul, 'So why don't you worship me rather than longing to worship me?' I stopped for a moment and did a double take. 'That's right, why don't I worship Him instead of just longing to do it?' I began to see that there may be many such things in life where we long to be right, rather than being right and going ahead and doing it for real. Was there a situation in our lives where we say the words but really we need to *do* and ***not just say***?

There are many ways that satan will try and influence people to go a different route which sounds good but actually goes nowhere. In fact as with this example, it takes us to a good feeling but it doesn't let us actually worship God. Ok I'm sure there is some little nugget in there but we can miss so much if we don't stick to real words to worship a real God.

I don't know about you but I want a full relationship with God. I know from His reputation that He is a wonderful and great God and I want to know Him better. I remember on one occasion saying to God, I want to know more about you. What do you like?, what do you think? What makes you tick?

Faith - The Working Factors

Some time later I read the scripture, that 'Without faith, we cannot please God', **so I wanted more faith exercised from there onwards to please Him.** It's important that we get to the matter of all things that support righteousness and create faith and do the miraculous. It sorts the right from the wrong when we see goodness performed and not just spoken of.

The people of the world need to see action in the church, not just preaching. Young people need to hear of a real God that defeats their enemies and heals the sick and sets people who are captive, free. If ever the believers in the churches needed a practical vision of who they are, it's in today's world. Drugs won't 'do it for them', neither will drink or pornography or half-hearted relationships, and they know that but there isn't any other life but God's life that will and someone needs to show them and not just tell them.

Practical Christianity is what the world needs, the type that General Booth of the Salvation Army lived, and the type that Peter and John had when they approached the man at the gate Beautiful in Jerusalem as they said, "Silver and gold have we

Faith - The Working Factors

don't have but such as we **do** have, ***we give you, rise up and walk!"***

It's easy to get caught up in a church where we do nothing practical and we let everyone else 'get on with it'. Determining to do God's will and read what He wants done for people and then ***doing it*** is what thrills us and sees people changed. God is **alive** and we as His people must be alive too or His gospel will be lost in the fog of this world.

And satan knows that. It's why he creates so many distractions to take people away from church and the good news of the gospel. It's why he attempts to hide the truth and seduce people's minds away from the life of God's words and God's Spirit. Satan knows that if the truth will get out and the reality is seen, he is defeated and beaten and his ways will be seen to fail.

Entertainment is a huge distraction these days. It takes up our time and we spend our days in fiction and entertaining music *that has no life to it.* But spend an evening in a church where the sick are prayed for and people are set free from their problems and you will see another life completely.

Faith - The Working Factors

Listen to what happens when believers tell you of what really happened when they trusted God in their crises and how they overcame their troubles, when they were healed of their sicknesses and their debts were cancelled, when their children were blessed and successful….. Listen as they tell you that they were delayed from leaving the house one day and just down the road in that moment there was fatal crash that would have happened when they got there. Listen as they tell you that they forgave their family for the way they abused them and then were instantly healed of their sickness. There are so many powerful stories of what God did in people's lives. Listen to George Muller's story as he prays for food for their orphanage and a knock comes on the door and there's a sack of flour sitting there on the doorstep or a local baker knocks the door to tell him that God kept him up all night worrying about the children of the orphanage and he just had to come and bring them bread.

God is real, the stories are real, the life waiting for us is real, let's not live another weak, powerless life when we can have an exciting existence that helps so many people.

Faith - The Working Factors

Are we being seduced away from goodness and right-ness? Is our faith life being thwarted and made stale by satan's discouraging ways? Are we being told that we could never be missionaries or that it's pointless speaking to people about Jesus, that nothing will happen to them, or that it's pointless laying hands on sick people, that's only supposed to be done by the super spiritual believers and only for the Pastors of the church. Do you see how we are being seduced into different thinking?

God has *real* faith for us to see working and useful faith *that is already in us waiting to be used.* We need to lose the idea that we are losers and that we have no faith. Our heavenly Father has all sorts of miracles lined up if we trust Him and believe what He says.

Jesus says, "The kingdom of God is *within you*".
He says, *"If you believe in me*, out of your innermost being will flow rivers of living water".
He says, "With God all things are possible and if *you believe* all things are possible".
He says, *"Have faith in God"*.
God still says, *"I am the Lord that Heals you"*.

Faith - The Working Factors

God is our creator, ***He is still our refuge and strength***.
God doesn't change, He still and always will have the same values. If He saved His people in the old testament, ***He will always save those who cry out to Him***.
He is trustworthy. ***So trust Him***.

We can look in other directions and be seduced into apathy about God and the faith that He gave us as satan wants us to do but have we really fully trusted this God who never fails? He said to Joshua just like He did to Moses before him, "***I will not fail you or forsake you***".
He never failed Daniel, He never failed the three Hebrew lads, He never failed Noah and his family and all the others we read of in scripture. He proved his loyalty to us when Jesus went to the cross to die in our place.
The wonderful picture to see is where young Isaac steps down off the altar of sacrifice and another takes his place. He is untied and set free, the knife is put down and the fire put on hold. Another takes his place on the altar. For us, that's Jesus, He took our place, He took *our* blame and *our*

Faith - The Working Factors

sicknesses. He loves us with an everlasting love. God provided *Himself* as a lamb.

The bible talks of us '***Holding fast to that which is good***. That means us not being seduced into another way, a second way, a double minded way. It means us being single minded and without any doubts about God.

Chapter 20
Faith – Rivers of Life

The words of Jesus give us a promise that we need. In John 7:38 Jesus says.

"He who believes in Me, as the Scripture has said, out of his innermost being will flow rivers of living water."

There is also another scripture that I want to align with this one.

It's found in Revelation chapter 22.

'And he shewed me a pure river of water of life, clear as crystal, proceeding out of the throne of God and of the Lamb. In the midst of the street of it, and on either side of the river, was there the tree of life, which bare twelve manner of fruits, and yielded her fruit every month: and the leaves of the tree were for the healing of the nations'.

Faith is an 'event changing' substance that changes bad to good, sickness to healing, unsafe to safe and death to life. It's clean and holy and pure. It's all to do with altering the vulnerable to safety and life. Just look at the disciples in the boat on the lake during the angry storm, after Jesus calmed the

Faith - The Working Factors

storm, he asks them, "Why is it you have so little faith, why do you have so much fear?"

Jesus **stops** the storm. He speaks out calm and safety and they are safe once more. We need to believe in Him wholeheartedly, we need the fruits of faith.

Once we align with Jesus, the faith begins to *flow*.

Look at the word Jesus speaks to us, "***If you believe***, Out of your innermost being shall **flow** rivers of living water".

In Heaven, there is a throne. A throne denotes dominion and power and authority. John describes it as we have read, 'A *pure river of water of life, clear as crystal, proceeding out of the throne of God and of the Lamb.*' Now there is a throne in us, it is the seat of our authority, our being, our place where we rule. But Jesus is saying, "If you believe in me"… if you accept my way and transfer your beliefs to my ways, put belief in you that now conforms to my thinking, then *out of you* will flow rivers of living water.

Faith - The Working Factors

The origin of that flow is the throne in Heaven. It is an origin where all life begins. God is our origin, He is **meant** to be where all our power comes from. So believing, - putting into our minds and hearts the originator of our beings, the full life of God creates *a well* of life in us. It's really faith, *alive, moving, flowing life*, to change our situations. And Jesus says if you put the idea of me, the notion of who I am into your belief system, then out of your spirit, your innermost being will *flow* RIVERS of LIVING water.

The life comes from where God's dominion originates, from Himself, from His throne, from His being, His Spirit. We align with Him, we agree with Him about who He is and in us begins a flow, a source we never had before, a well of life springing up delivering faith to everywhere we need it. It's the life nature of the Almighty that created us in the beginning, re introducing Himself to us when we believe in this man Jesus.

Who is Jesus? He is God, He came and lived as a man among us and showed His dominion power in everything He did. Watch as He turns water into wine, as He heals the sick, cleanses the lepers, He

Faith - The Working Factors

raises dead people up and speaks to the elements, calming storms and filling nets with fish after men have laboured all night and caught nothing. He is a fountain of life who makes dead things live and thrive. This is not just a throne, a seat in heaven, this is the person of God, the origin of all life that pulsates with truth and life Spirit. This is Almighty God.

What Jesus says to put in our hearts is Himself, 'Believe in **me**', He says, put your belief in my being and learn who I am. Then once that revelation comes alive in you, it will grow and invigorate you and flow out of you to all around you. That is what faith is. It is the flowing power of God alive in us that changes dead situations to live ones.

"Believe in Me". Let your soul catch the breath of life that makes you alive. Put into the heart of you, your very soul, the principles of overcoming power that life is. **"Believe in me!"**

"If you believe in me, *out of your innermost being shall flow rivers of living water."*
Just believe for it.

Faith - The Working Factors

Faith starts when we believe. We open the door to God and put in our souls the concept of what He is. We let in the Holy Spirit and accept the whole idea of Him, we open our doors and windows to God and let Him roam through us, giving Him free access to all of our being. We surrender to Him, we *believe*.

Accepting the wonderful chain reaction of His life in us makes us grow and develop. Faith takes up its proper place again and does all the things we need it to do. We were meant for full life to abide in us. That life is God.

Faith - The Working Factors

Chapter 21
"BY Faith…."

The above phrase is saying that things happen when we use faith. Whether it's something we need that we know God can supply or whether it's something that is troubling us that we need dealt with, Faith, the inheritance of God is the answer. We can think outside of God or we can include Him and His special ways and see all manner of answers come to us and solve our problems.

We were never taught in this world to have the answers to everything but God, as Job said, IS the answer to everything, - "I know that you can do ***everything***". When we believe Him, we start seeing it and problems are sorted. All of Job's issues were dealt with <u>as soon as he declared and confessed it.</u> You have to confess it. **Salvation starts with a confession.** "If you believe in your heart ***and*** confess with your mouth… You shall be saved". You can believe it inside you but when you declare it, the life of the declaration begins.

So many in scripture made statements to Jesus declaring their belief, even declaring that they

181

Faith - The Working Factors

wanted help with their *unbelief* and Jesus healed them. **The faith road STARTS with belief.** We hear, we receive hope from *what* we hear and then ***we believe*** and ***declare*** that we believe and the salvation is there.

Faith is what we **see**. Hope is what we understand we can have when someone tells us that God can do anything. We then believe for it and set the matter in the concrete of God's promise. We fix it firm in our conscious mind that God said it and we believe Him. Look again at what I said in the Bible college dormitory that night.... "You said it Lord, I believe it, now I'm going to sleep" and against the odds, I slammed my head on the pillow and shut my eyes… and slept! We align ourselves with God's words, - scripture; in other words, what God said via the prophets or via Jesus or via the Apostles. We get our belief that way, we get our hope that way, it's made alive in us. Then we go ahead, we hold out for the faith to happen, that moment when the *substance* of what we *hoped* for is actually seen and lives in front of us.

The remedy is produced ***by faith***.

Faith - The Working Factors

The production line is called Hope, belief, **faith**. It is the life power that produces. You can follow the stages along the production line of belief and hope. The precepts, the principles of faith, are built into you by the hope of what God says and people add their testimonials of what God did in their lives and you see the picture of the remedy and then you act.... And then FAITH lives. The *substance* of what you hoped for *arrives*. BY faith it happens. John said in his gospel, the *Word* became **flesh** and lived among us and we *saw* His glory. Then He was alive in our midst, the salvation we were waiting for, the Glory of God. The copious presence of the Almighty, Jesus, was there just as He was promised to us.

You see, it's no different seeing Jesus in the flesh as it is seeing your remedy, your healing, your miracle appear. You're seeing God's answer standing there. He became flesh and stood there in your midst. A live answer from the Father.

So pray and wait and expect for the answer.

Faith - The Working Factors

Through Faith. 'By grace you are saved through faith'. Grace is the gift of God, Faith is the nature you were born again with to do the saving.

Chapter 22
Faith - the LIFE Factor

As I walked the dog this morning, I had to entice myself to do it. I'm a retired person now (well that's what they call us when we finish work and take our pension). It's not always easy to get out of bed and face another day, the bed is warm and in the U.K in November that's a good reason to stay there. It's comfortable, it's pleasant and I can just lie there, to meditate and think. I can muse about this book and all the other revelation that God gives me. But then, the dog needs his walk. I have things that need to be done. Whether old or young, we all have these moments.

As I thought of the day, I had every reason, in my mind, to let the day go and chill out. Very recently, I lost my wife, during a battle with cancer and doubt and fear and all the other factors against us, we strove, with the word of God against this awful disease. We made a pact together from the first diagnosis to just believe for her healing. It surprised me, after seeing the pains disappear every time we prayed and after many high level battles with pain and the very difficult

Faith - The Working Factors

chemotherapy and sepsis which she appeared to receive while in the cancer hospital and after many physical setbacks with various drugs and after seeing her beginning to eat again and get stronger; it was a surprise that that one morning I couldn't rouse her. A friend of ours told us that during the night God had woken him to pray for Helen, that she would have peace.

That morning, very peacefully, my love had gone. So I lost her to Heaven. My loss (well not really, my biggest consolation is that she is enjoying seeing Jesus). God's and her gain.

I had gone through a period of mourning and great sadness at my loss and the family's loss. She was a great mother and a wonderful wife. As I tried to get away from things in the house, going out to the garage and workshop to try and escape all the recent poor memories, I looked around at all my tools and the evidence of years of DIY and house repair, I realised that ever since I had met her, all that I did was for her and our home. My reason to be, *in the natural world,* had gone.

Faith - The Working Factors

It was just about that time that God spoke to me. "I have given you the oil of joy for mourning and the garments of praise for the spirit of heaviness", He relayed to me from the Old Testament. God had given to me the oil of joy *for* my mourning. I had, wrapped around me garments of praise to use *for* my spirit of heaviness. Now don't get me wrong, that day we lost her I had great peace and strength from the Almighty. I had many questions as well of course about why *my* faith hadn't seemed to work but of course it *had* worked, every time we prayed, the pain went and God answered me. In the hospital when she wasn't at home where we *could* pray (for quite long periods), she had pain and they gave her an opiate drug to kill the pain and that took the edge off her thinking and I believe, to some degree weakened her resolve somewhat, maybe. We *need* our minds and our wills free to focus on God and for the focus not to be taken away. I want to make it clear, I don't believe in any way we *lost* the fight; she is in glory now with no pain and triumphant in soul and spirit. Did faith fail? To me, *no*.

It seems the fight was taken out of my hands and she went home where it seems God wanted her.

Faith - The Working Factors

But now, here I am without my soul mate of 50 years and what am I to do? She had been a big answer to *my* needs and *I* to hers. Many were the times we lifted each other and prayed when we were sick and saw miracles happen. <u>We had a life of faith and miraculous events.</u> She and I pulled together with missions to Africa and projects to support children there and Pakistan. *Now,* there was just me.

But Faith is the *substance* we need for life. Faith is the LIFE FORCE of God that takes us *forward* and makes us *live* even when we have been depleted of the stable things in life, even our life's loves.

God reminded me again today of some scriptures. Do we let lethargy set in because there seems to be a loss now in our lives and it's hard to go on? Do we let sloth (that deadly sin) creep into our lives masquerading as the right to give up because there's no impetus to go on any more? Did Jesus just give up on the road to the cross? No. *He* went on **so that** *we* could go **on**. He is the author of Faith. Scripture says, (KJV) "We have the faith *of* Christ". Once we are born again, we have in us

Faith - The Working Factors

the Spirit of the living God, we go through the waters of baptism and bury that old person that we were and it's deeds, with Jesus in His death and *rise* in newness of life. Is my life over? NO. It is risen with Him by the power of the Holy Spirit, the one who raised Him from the dead.

Do I have to concede now and lay down my life because my reason to be in the natural has gone to Heaven? Certainly not. I have no idea at this time what God will yet do with me in the years to come, what adventures we will yet have together. I have seen sinners forgiven both here in UK, and in Uganda Africa, in Ukraine, Kenya and Rwanda and the sick healed and miracles done. Why should this *ever* be the end? If God is anything in my mind, He is the one *who was* and *is* and *is to come*, the Almighty.

Now don't get me wrong, I have lost my wife to cancer, *or have I*? *No, I lost her to Heaven*. Cancer is *not* the reason she is in Heaven. Her salvation is the reason she is now with Jesus in Heaven. He bought her with a great price, paid for her salvation and all the miracles she saw. He gave her all the wonderful things she had during

Faith - The Working Factors

her life, she would tell you of them if she were here. She had a tremendous faith and *it worked.* So we cannot dwell on this episode. Was it loss? No. It is a victory, she is in Heaven. During her life she encouraged all of us to live and put down sickness and fear. *That's not failure*.

You see, there are things in scripture that tell us not to be slothful, not to be lazy but strive and go forward, to live and not die, to have faith, the sort that can move mountains! It's at times like this that the thoughts of the resurrection of Jesus lifts us when we need lifting. Those resurrection notions and inspirations carry us *up* and *out* of our situations.

This is where the resurrecting power of God really counts. When we are in failure mode having been set back by events, then we succeed with God's powerful Spirit in us. "If *the same Spirit* that raised Jesus from the dead dwells in *you*, He *shall also* make alive *your* mortal bodies BY that Spirit." Romans 8:11… and that goes for your mind and your emotions too.

Faith - The Working Factors

His resurrection is ***our*** resurrection too. Have you got some downturn in your life that needs burying? Then bury it and rise with Jesus in newness of life. The dog needs walking, the sick need healing, the sinners need forgiveness and release from their horrible lives. ***Faith is here to do all of that***, not to allow us to fail and go down in despair. God nor faith is not the author of despair and failure, any more than He is the author of death. God is the creator, the **maker** and author of LIFE not the destroyer of it.

Faith is life, it's the ***substance in us*** we see that is vibrant and active after satan has tried to pull us down and depress us. ***This*** mortal *can* put on immortality **now** and this corrupted being that I was before I got born again *can* put on incorruption ***now***. The resurrection has already happened. It happened when Jesus ROSE from the dead and when I got baptised, I did the same as Jesus did, ***I rose too with Him***. In my spirit, I felt it when I got born again even though I had not yet been baptised. The life of God came in right then when I invited Him and His Spirit took me up out of my sin. His blood's life made me clean and alive in righteousness.

Faith - The Working Factors

You see, our failures don't count any more. Jesus rising from out of death into fullness of life is what counts *because when He rose, all believers rose.* We rose out of our lethargy and our weaknesses and our sloth, out of our depression and gloom, out of our darkness and into HIS light. So, let there be light! God speaks it into our hearts, **Faith - our working factor.** God's *factor*y is at work making our lives new and full of His life.

Let's see the full power of Faith. Let's have all the right factors. Let's recognise the real active power of faith and accept the reality of it. God is right here to make you alive to it and to put down the fear, the failure, the sickness and the weakness, the inability to rise and the laziness that we often have that stops us rising. The God of resurrecting power is right here if you will accept His fullness and surrender all your life to Him.

Chapter 23
Faith – Pleasing the Father

I always remember being in Church as the worship there was rising to a wonderful crescendo one Sunday morning. We sang that lovely hymn by Charles Wesley that includes the words …,
"Changed from glory into glory, till in Heaven we take our place, *till we cast our crowns before Him, lost in wonder love and praise."* I was lost in the sheer praise of the moment and feeling the goodness of God. There was a sense of Heaven about the church that morning and God's presence was just there, right among us. A Holy moment and a moment when you wanted to give all your heart to Him. All that Jesus had done on that awful cross had redeemed us and healed us and you just wanted to abandon any other thoughts and imagine Jesus, the lamb of God, the one who gave His whole being for you to save you. But after singing it I thought, 'What do I want with a crown?' I haven't done anything, **He did it all**, *for me*. I have no crown, He is the Lord of all and I'm not much beside Him.

Faith - The Working Factors

After a while I reflected on that moment and then I began to wonder why would *we* have crowns? I knew of the book of Revelation where John sees the crowns of the twenty four elders being cast at Jesus' feet. But why should *we* have crowns? The scripture talks too about there being a crown of glory being given to those who overcome, to those who persevere. I didn't want a crown, and I smarted a bit inside at the thought. Me, with a crown? No. I felt ridiculous at the thought. But Jesus had done so much for me, He had saved my soul, He had healed me, He had so often saved my life, and in that atmosphere of worship where everyone was praising Him, I did too but I had shunned the thought of having a crown.

But I felt a bit naked now, where *was* my crown? What had I done for Him? He had done so much for me but what did ***I*** do for ***Him?***

All of a sudden, I felt broken and emotional. I was a taker, not a giver. I now needed a crown so that I had one to cast at His feet in praise. All of a sudden ***I*** needed a crown. I needed to serve Him properly and really do something *for Him,* he loved me and deserved more than just praise. I

Faith - The Working Factors

needed to do something deserving of a crown. *I needed a crown*. A crown would please my Father in Heaven.

Scripture says that without 'Faith we cannot please God'. Praise *is* our crowning glory, somehow it was something that I could never freely do. I connected the dots as they say and began to realise that I must be a *better* son, a *better* testimonial of my father's goodness to me, a *better* likeness of His. The world needs to see who He is and how good He is and I was hiding Him from them.

You know, we can hide from who we are. We can keep hidden inside us the life that God has given us. We often do it out of fear or out of self-consciousness or simply out of the embarrassment that our old nature generates in us, that we were a lost people and no good. But all that is gone, salvation gives us robes of righteousness and God's armour. We are new creatures now, there is nothing to be embarrassed or self-conscious about or fearful for. We are God's children now and we must not be lacking in goodness after all that Jesus has done for us.

Faith - The Working Factors

Sometimes it takes a deep commitment from us and we often fear that we can't do that but all the time, inside us is a new person just waiting to be let out of its chains. Let me tell you, the chains are GONE. Take a look, a real look, the chains you thought you had are not there anymore. So step out, take a deep breath, go forward and do the things Jesus *said we could do*. It's Faith time; it's time to believe *who we are* and *what* we can do *if* we believe.

If you want to please God, you can. Just follow what Jesus says. He knows how to please the Father, so just do what *He* does and copy Him. We do that in life don't we? We see what pleases our parents and if we are good children, we do what they like us to do and we often get rewarded for it. We copy others and see what Mum or Dad enjoy. We get their favourite chocolates for their birthday or their favourite food or clothes but best of all they like to see us grow up and be decent people, so maybe, just maybe we will be that, right?

My parents were God fearing, good people and I tried to do what was right for their sake. They

Faith - The Working Factors

were kind and generous but *I* wasn't always that. But there came a time when God changed my heart and I began to want to be better. I heard my father talk of his healing of being a stammerer and how good God was to him giving him food when he had none as a young man and was out of work. I started to want to be like him and then my life changed, bit by bit, little by little. I saw some changes and I knew that my Heavenly Father would now be better pleased.

I remember wanting to go to Bible College, not to study and be a theologian but to give God time to get *to* me and explore my heart and I wanted to get to know Him and know what He thought. I knew I couldn't devote much proper time to Him while I worked and my father paid my fees while in Bible College so that I could do God's things.

That was the turning point between my weak days and my strong days. I had many things to overcome but they were all dealt with. God got me a new woman in my life who became my wife and slowly my faith grew. She taught me how to not fear and was a great example to me in so many ways. The right partner in life is so important so I

Faith - The Working Factors

prayed and asked God to send me the right one and He gave me Helen not long after. We were together for over 50 years.

God will give you all that you need once you decide to do what is right in His sight. Jesus said, "Seek *first* what is right and *seek **God's Kingdom***, (not *your* kingdom) and *all the things* that the unbelievers seek after, will be ***given*** you!" That's not difficult. Just do what is right.

A lot of people can't see how to please God or get their faith working but the solution is really quite simple. Just do what is right. Be kind, be helpful, be good like your Father in Heaven, clothe the naked, feed the hungry, do it in Jesus' name so that He gets the praise for it. Preach the gospel, remind people that Almighty God is here to save them and help them. Tell them how He saved you and that He can also save them.

When I went back to Uganda after going there the first time, I knew in my heart that I had to preach there, so I asked God what He wanted me to say to the people of Uganda. His response took me aback as He very clearly and vociferously said to me,

Faith - The Working Factors

interrupting me, mid-sentence, **"Tell My people they are forgiven"**. *Wow,* did that sink in? Yes it did, it got my attention. *Well, I did ask.* In no uncertain terms God told me what mattered to Him. He wanted me to tell His people that they were forgiven. Everywhere I went that year I preached forgiveness. He supplied all the venues and I preached this new message that He gave me. He taught me forgiveness and I found out that when you forgive, you release a prisoner but ***you*** are the prisoner that gets released! Everywhere I preached it, people got saved, around 350 in ten days or so. I was simply astonished. I got home after the mission and received the news that about 200 young people gave their lives to God after I had preached in a school. I simply sat and cried.

If you want to please God, just do as He says and He will bless you. ***All*** the things that the unbelievers seek after will be ***given*** to you. It's not rocket science, this is much more powerful than rocket science, seeing lives changed and people healed who have had back pain for years and those with strokes healed. God wants to be pleased and we need to please Him. 'God works in you to will and to do of His good pleasure', -

Faith - The Working Factors

when you obey Him. I always thought that it was difficult to do the will of God. It's easier than I thought, - you just obey Him. Oh yes, satan makes out you'll have all sorts of trials and tribulations 'but God delivers us out of them all!' See that? - ***God has the answer to everything***, even if you don't.

Just please Him. Use your faith. Do what Jesus ***says*** to do… **"Have Faith in God"**….. "If ***you*** have faith (and we all have 'the measure of faith') you will ***say*** to all the mountains that are in your way, ***"Move and be cast into the sea"*** (In other words, get out of my sight) and they will obey you!" Why does He pick on such a **big** object? Because FAITH can REMOVE the BIGGEST things in your way.

That is the message of this book…. Have Faith in your Father in Heaven. You can do all things through Christ who strengthens you. The scriptures back up all the Faith ventures you take up. There are words of power and courage just waiting for you to discover them. God always backs you up and watches over your works. The secret is to fully trust Him, He always delivers on His promises.

Faith - The Working Factors

Chapter 24
So what is this book about?

IT IS about faith. How you get better working faith. It's about how to get rid of the things that destroy your faith or minimise it. It's about getting rid of the doubts and *what* doubt is. It is about human people who, although having sunk in despair and thought themselves to be useless when it comes to using faith, can find in fact that they have faith after all and it's not hard to use it, you just have to trust God. The book is about doing just that, believing what He says and doing what He says to do and strangely, it works. It's about learning who you are and that God is bigger than you thought He was and it follows that if you are born again, remade to be like Him, then you are bigger than you thought you were. It's about seeing yourself as God's child now, no longer a waster and good for nothing, you are actually in real terms, a new creature. This book like all of the Bible is telling you that you don't have to run from any giant or any sickness or any demon power or satan himself even, it is telling you, as Jesus told us, "I give you power over all the power of the enemy!" This book is informing you that

Faith - The Working Factors

you have dominion power like Adam had, that once born again, recreated again like the Almighty, you have power over every creeping thing. Mountains move for you now and whereas you would have run away if satan said 'boo', now you say politely (or impolitely, it's up to you now) "NO! , I'm in charge of my affairs now, in Jesus name". You are a different creature now. Now you say, "I am who God says I am!"

This book should tell you what the Bible says, that God is on your side, He is not against you, He is *for* you. You, like Elijah have a small cave to run into away from the winds and the earthquakes and the burning fires where you can listen to God's still small voice that says to you, "You're ok, you're with me, trust me, relax, fear not".

This book should be telling you that you can do all things now through Christ, the anointing of God's Spirit that is in you. He's there, right there, in your innermost being, waiting until you need Him.

This book should be telling you, once again, like the Bible, that with your faith you can still storms and pray for the sick and that they will recover,

Faith - The Working Factors

like Jesus said they would. If it doesn't, then I've failed. Can I say, that if any book doesn't increase your faith, or get you to believe better or hope better, then get a better book. God's aim is to make you live and be an increased person in terms of right-ness and goodness and to be more like Him.

The God of resurrection, that great Spirit that raised Jesus from death is *here* to make you better in every way. Paul says, "Try all the spirits, that is, put them on trial to see whether they are of God or not, and if they are not then push them away. What you need is the Spirit of God that will raise you, lift you, better you and make you a greater person, more loving, kinder, more joyful, more peaceful, more like Jesus. The world can make you more resentful or malicious, more judgemental and bitter. We need better, in God's way, better.

This book should be telling you that when Jesus went to the cross, *He did it for you*. He died *for* your transgressions, He was wounded *for* them to be forgiven. He was bruised *for* your unfairness, to make you just and fair minded. He was chastised, punished in your place, *so that* you can

Faith - The Working Factors

have peace. He was lashed with the Roman Flagrum, the cat of nine tails and whipped *so that* you can be healed. This book is about the reality of what God thinks about you and what He did for you to be better in your spirit, in your soul and in your body. He has full healing for you. When He made us in the beginning, He made us with full life. He never intended for us to be anything other than that. It was satan and man's poor choices that made us lesser and poorer. God wants to bring us back to full maturity and full strength. If other books tell you differently, then consign them to the rubbish heap. God wants you well and fit and thinking right, all the time. We are richer than that old way of thinking. We are the children of the God that says, "Be fruitful and multiply and replenish the earth". That's His way.

Faith is God's way. Faith is life. Whenever you need an answer, Faith is there in you. That's what this book is about.

So what is *your* book about? What is your life saying? Who is reading you? Who's turning your pages and reading your content? What is your heart all about? Peel back the cover and look

Faith - The Working Factors

under the flyleaf and see who this believer is. We can see what the cover says and the advertisements say but what does the book say inside, what's the core of the message? What's the reality? What is *my* book about, what am I telling with my life?

Our lives are what God made them to be in the beginning but the message has been messed with by satan, by the world and by our own flesh which receives all the nonsense knowledge from around it. Who the world is, has been covered in darkness and its message is now a dark message where danger lurks and disease lingers all the time, ***unless*** <u>we change it and transfer the emphasis</u> of the way things have become, to another emphasis. The Gospel of Jesus will do this. Where people once died before, they can now change and we see them healed, ***by faith***.

It starts when we believe the book. Not my book only but the Bible and the truth God filled it with. My book is just a re-iteration of His book. His book starts with how things were in the beginning, it continues on from, 'Let there be light' to 'Let there be salvation' and healing and wealth and dominion' for all those who read it with belief.

Faith - The Working Factors

We need to read with belief, looking for the faith changing that occurs within its pages. We need to see where and how God intervenes to destroy the wrong and bring in the life. It begins with a readable narrative that says all the time, "Out with the old way and in with God's way." It's what we do with our lives, our book. We present the story of what we are, what God has done in us and how we used to be before He changed us.

What is our book about? How do we tell our story? I know what David's story is about, what Daniel's story is, what Peter's story is about, what Paul's story is about, their stories are all about change, real change, the change that faith makes. The *evidence* of faith is the change, the *substance* of what happened when they all believed God. The giants fell, the lions mouths were shut, the fish poured into the empty net and the water held their weight when they walked on it and the world was changed. ***These are the vital factors of the book.*** They are vital to the world if the world is to be changed.

Faith - The Working Factors

Chapter 25
Courage –Seeing what we have

We don't all seem to have courage, many display a weak attitude and quiet ways that are not aggressive but at the same time are not courageous but instead give in to challenges. Not having courage stops us doing the essential things that must be done sometimes to get our life back on track after an assault of some kind.

Faith often requires us to stand up and be counted when attacks of the enemy, when satan and his kingdom, come against us. ***We need to remember a few things though.*** **Firstly**, Faith comes from God and is part of our born again nature; it therefore follows that we have in us the ability to overcome all manner of problems and personalities that come against us, simply because God's nature is more powerful than all. **Secondly**, God commitment to us is a powerful one and never lets us down. Remember God's words to Joshua in Joshua Chapter one, "I will never leave you nor forsake you, as I was with Moses, so I will be with you". For you and me, that means His commitment to get us through troubles is the same

Faith - The Working Factors

as any of God's people. All it takes from us is to surrender to His ways and His thinking. Both Moses and Joshua put themselves into God's hands and let God do with them what He would. That's surrender of the right kind because God will not let you down, that's a given.

Not many realise that giving your life into God's hands is the most powerful and authoritative thing you can do. If you don't seem to have the wherewithal to go out and conquer, then how about putting yourself in the hands of someone who can. ***God is just that person.*** He is the Almighty God, your Heavenly Father. Its personal with Him, He is your Father in the finest sense of the phrase and He's always on your side, so rest in your relationship with Him, He will get you all the courage you need when you need it.

Strength of mind and heart are the most powerful assets when you employ them.

'Courage' comes from the Latin word for heart, 'Cor'. , *'Couer' in French.* King Richard of England was known as Richard Couer de lyon, the heart of the Lion. Sometimes we need to reach

Faith - The Working Factors

within us and pull out and use the character of God that we got when we became born again. **We have Courage.** We got it when we were born-again. We just have to know it and employ it, - to use it.

We can get very tied up with the world's use of words. I see the weak use of the word 'encourage; often these days. "Oh let's encourage one another!" 'Encouragement' seems to have come away from the fact of true courage. I heard some say, "Let's go and encourage some people to....". The Lord spoke to me just then and I turned to them and said, 'Can I just stop you there,… Just go out and give them courage!" Their eyes lit up as they got the message from the Lord. "Yes, I get it," one of them said, "Let's go and *give* courage." Their actions showed that they were newly resolved to pick up the weak and strengthen them.

I get the impression that our 'core', our spirit, that born again part of us that is re-created in God's image when we got born-again, is the part that contains God's powerful nature. It's just that many of us haven't become aware of it yet. Our 'Core', our inner-man, our spirit, is now renewed and has a whole new ability after receiving

Faith - The Working Factors

forgiveness from God and after we invited Him into our beings. I am not the old Terry Leaman that I was, I have God's courage now, I face challenges with His Spirit in me and with His courage. I don't back off any more when satan growls, instead I think of David facing that giant, striding out to meet this challenger who is calling God's people names. 'Who does he think he is?' Instead of running away, I listen to scripture (Romans 8) "I am more than a conqueror through Him that loves me!" See, now, *that's who I am*.

We need to appreciate that if we stay as we have always been, we'll run away at the first sign of a challenge but if we listen to what our Father in Heaven tells us, we'll get another picture. Failure is not for us, not when we have such a Father God who is inspiring us to overcome all things. He stands behind us and backs us in all that we do that is good and right. He always did for all of those who took courage and stated whose side they were on. **And sometimes that is what is needed**.

We need to simply say with strength, "I am on the Lord's side!" I like to watch what David did and his attitude was when everyone else was terrified

Faith - The Working Factors

by the giant. David was obviously indignant and full of courage when He knew that God would always back him up. Instead of being fearful, he ran towards the giant and proclaimed who his God was, preparing to destroy this challenger of the armies of the living God. That's who we are. COURAGE. God's courage in us, doing the work it is supposed to do.

I have seen God's courage rise in my soul on occasions when trouble arises. I have seen it bear witness to who I am as the Spirit of God calls me to rise up and face the enemy. My friends, <u>we do not have to run or fail</u>, we are God's children. I remember one day when I came home early from working away, my son was running to meet me in the drive of our house. "Dad, come quick, mummy's ill, she can't breathe and she's talking funny", he told me. As I went up to the bedroom she lay there unable to breathe and was delirious, I couldn't understand her. There was no time to call for the doctor or an ambulance, so I got the little bottle of oil that we used when we prayed for the sick and put some oil on her and prayed, telling the sickness to leave her. In 2 minutes, she opened her eyes and spoke lucidly to me. Such was a time to

Faith - The Working Factors

have God's courage inside you and speak in courage. Calling the doctor later, he confirmed that she had pneumonia. And then rather unscripted, after watching her and listening to her chest with his stethoscope over a period, he confessed, "I have never seen Pneumonia getting better on its own before!" We have in our core, God's Spirit. I get the impression that the word, 'Core' is related to the word courage. At our core we have ***God's*** heart, His power, His initiative, His strength to do what is necessary when it needs to be done.

We are never abandoned to the world, God's Spirit is here in our midst, at our core. And God is not scared of anything. Remember that, when you are challenged. Tell me, think it out, do you think that Almighty God is afraid of anything? The answer is NO. Can anything suppress him or belittle Him? No. And His Spirit is in you to give you courage. One of the great factors of faith is this in-suppressible core of God that He has put in us at salvation. The Almighty God has installed in us His nature again, we got born AGAIN.

Faith - The Working Factors

God wants us to know that the ability we need is in us so get the confidence you need from what He says and put down the giants. You have the courage.

Faith - The Working Factors

Chapter 26
The Triune Factor

We need to consider all of God's being when we talk about Faith because we too are triune like Him and there lies our faith power as well as all of our new God like qualities. Being born again is being remade/recreated in our Father's image and likeness and being filled with His Spirit. If Adam was created this way, and he was, (read Genesis One to see how Adam was made of God's nature) then when we are **'Born-again'** we were *re-created.* The three parts of God had a direct part to play in our salvation, our rebirth process. We 1. Believed the words spoken by Jesus, we 2 Received His Spirit of truth and we 3 Responded to our Father's heart with our souls, somewhere with all of that we received the whole of God's character, albeit bit by bit as He came alive in us again and the rebirth took place. Ok, we needed to kill off the old person that we were and bury him/her in baptism and then rise in our new nature to be raised with Jesus in His resurrection.

So somewhere in our beings at the point of salvation, the new birth, there came a new set of rules and characteristics set alight by the Spirit of

Faith - The Working Factors

our Father in Heaven. We *became* new creatures in Christ Jesus. Old things passed away and all things became new.

Now I want you to see what happened with our Faith. In your Spirit Faith was reborn (as was all of your being). Just then in your soul the word of God became a reality, as Jesus said, 'You will speak to mountains in your way and move them' with your new thoughts. The Holy Spirit acts on that and does the moving of the mountain using your faith, the faith that has been newly established by the words of God within you.

All that we do with our new being uses God's nature to do it. Firstly the notion of what is needed to be done comes from our Fathers nature, the whole idea of good is His, it has a right way about it, a correct and proper manner and attitude. Secondly we hear of that right way from the words of God, spoken by the prophets and then from Jesus directly and then from the Apostles who spoke under the inspiration of God's Spirit. When

Faith - The Working Factors

we believed God's words we used our will to accept His principles and then to speak them ourselves. We put ourselves in line with God's ways and His power. This why, whenever people were on God's side, what they did was backed up by Him and it became an active event. God always demands that we believe and then speak what we believe, *then* it becomes an alive event and a reality. Notice that even God Himself speaks before it becomes a reality. In Genesis One God firstly 'thinks' it, then **Speaks**, "**Let there be**…. **Light**…. And light *became*. This is the principle that God demands that we use, Believe it, then Speak it into being. Watch as Jesus teaches it in Mark 11….. "*Have* faith in God… If you have faith you will *say* to this mountain … 'move' and it will obey you. Do you see the transition from inaction (hidden) to action (seen), all caused by faith. Firstly <u>believe</u> what God Himself says, then <u>speak</u> what God speaks, then see what God said would happen if you spoke it. It's a simple process but it does mean that you have to believe first. That's why we dealt with other subjects like, 'doubt' etc in previous chapters.

Faith - The Working Factors

I remember what Pat Robertson said one day on a CBN broadcast, "Follow the chain of command…. You pray, God the Father hears, He sends the command forward with the Holy Spirit, He communicates it to your spirit, you take the thought into your mind, and then by faith speak the word." The ***action*** takes place as if God Himself spoke it. Well in effect, He did; you are a child of God, you spoke in agreement with your Father's words and it happened just like He said it would. ***The mountain moved,*** whatever mountainous obstacle that was and it disappeared out of sight. It's God's prescribed way. Jesus said that's what would happen.

The whole of Jesus was crucified and died for all our ailments and wrongs, in order for our beings to be totally catered for. God is not someone who partly does a job; our God is a perfectionist. 'Full salvation, full salvation' pens the hymn writer and is the right perception to have. There is a perfectness about what God does in our salvation, a whole God is involved in securing a whole new being for us. We needed saving in all our being and He came Himself to do it.

Faith - The Working Factors

Watch the words of John 3:16 closely... "For God so loved the world, that He gave His only begotten son, that whoever believed on Him should not perish but have everlasting life. God's *heart* so loved you and then He gave his *son* so that if you process it, you will receive everlasting **Life, *His Spirit*.**

The *soul* of the Triune God, the Father, loved us and He gave us His *son*, His likeness, so that whoever believed on Him received His *Spirit*.

If a whole God does not redeem us, we are not fully redeemed because being made originally completely like Him, if we are not fully redeemed, we will never be what we were meant to be. But God doesn't let his perfect purpose slip, He comes Himself to ensure we become what He purposed us to be.

I believe that *we really need to know these things*, our confidence in God depends on it. After all the bombardment our race has taken from satan, from the world and from our degraded flesh, we need to be taught properly that God did something extraordinary to redeem us. It affects our faith,

Faith - The Working Factors

that if we see how many lengths He went to, in order to give us His full nature again, we will realise the extent of His stature in us.

Our faith is vital to not only *our* existence but the existence of *others*. We need to exercise our faith to show the substance of what God has put in us and the evidence of the possible that is made available by faith. We need to show that as Jesus said, with God all things are possible and if we believe all things will be possible again. **There are no closed doors to faith,** only to unbelief. Full working faith can make available any right thing that we need. A full God makes available the impossible to us. Others may struggle but the believer's faith makes it all happen.

God spoke to the world, His voice is Jesus. He told us that if we believe, anything is possible bar failure. God the father through Jesus told us how to do things, the Holy Spirit finishes the job when we believe it and speak it. The Trinity is all over the work when we speak in faith.

I remember the evangelist Peter Scothern telling how that he was waiting on God for the Holy Spirit

Faith - The Working Factors

but he was struggling to understand the concept of the trinity. God told him to get some oil and anoint himself and fast and pray. He searched the house for oil but could not find any. Finally, right up in the top of a cupboard he found some bicycle oil. As he lifted it down, he saw the name of the oil, '3 in 1'. It cleaned, it penetrated, and it lubricated. He anointed himself and his soul winning and healing ministry began. Not long ago I was musing on his story and as I went to clean my teeth that morning. I went into the draw of my bathroom sink unit for my toothpaste, I lifted up the tube of toothpaste and it read, 'Triple action'.

God wants to remind us that all of his being is behind our redemption and our personal power to do what is right. Behind your faith is the word of God, sent from the Father and empowered by the Holy Spirit. His whole character is the nature that powers your faith. He backs you all the way when you believe Him and use your faith.

I would also remind you of the terminology Jesus uses when a woman is healed, "Daughter, thy faith has made you ***whole***". Jesus is saying that up to this point you were not ***fully*** well but your faith

Faith - The Working Factors

has made you '**whole**'. A complete God made her *complete* again. When errors have crept into our body, souls and spirits we are disjointed, broken, unable as we say, to 'pull things together'. We are not complete and working properly but God wants us perfect. The meaning of perfect is complete. Full health is often rendered 'wholeness'. '*Perfect*' means 'as good as it is possible to be', 'completely free from error or fault'.

Unbroken is what God wants us to be but Jesus was broken for us to be made whole, repaired if you like. Only our creator can remake us back to our original specification. There have been times when my car has been faulty and the local garage has been unable to put it right, that I have had to take it to the manufacturer's garage, to his agent to have the experts look at it. Only the manufacturer has the answer to fix some faults. Only *they* know how the car was built and put together.

Knowing our creator and the intricate knowledge He has about us, is the wisdom we need when we are damaged and need renewing. As somebody said, 'If God made us, surely we can trust Him with our repairs'. Often though, God is the last

Faith - The Working Factors

one we go to for help. ***He should be the first***. When my wife was very ill, when I had come home and found her in bed, delirious and unable to breathe, there was no time to call for a doctor. I immediately called out to God. I put oil on her (oil is the symbol of the Holy Spirit) and prayed and told the sickness to go. In about two minutes she opened her eyes and her speech was normal again. Until then her breathing was noisy and her speech was unintelligent, she was rambling. We then called the doctor whose *immediate* diagnosis was that she had Pneumonia and must go to hospital but in the time that the ambulance took to come he listened repeatedly at intervals to her chest. Then he declared, "I don't understand it, I have seen Pneumonia many times but I have never seen it getting better on its own before!"

THE doctor, her creator had already been summoned to her bedside and He had already acted. I was so glad that we called the doctor though, simply to get that statement from him. He volunteered it, it was a lovely confirmation that God had already worked His work.

Faith - The Working Factors

A full God meets our full needs because He is our originator, our creator, He knows everything about us. All the *working* factors come from HIM.

Faith - The Working Factors

Chapter 27
The DOMINION of Faith

We have talked of the superiority of God's ways encased in the salvation God has given us and we need to keep considering them all and what we really have when we get Born-Again.

The world, satan and the things of the world that have spoken into our flesh and been stored in our minds, have dulled our senses to who we are and what we can do as new creatures in Christ. But make no mistake, Jesus has picked us out, every one of us, to be the people He first created. He never had a plan to make us second rate or for us to take orders from any unrighteous being or system. *He always spoke and told us to rise.* Fishermen became fishers of *men*, the lame people now *walked*, the blind people *saw*, the dead *rose up* in front of him and paralysed people *got up and carried their beds home*.

What God gave Adam in the beginning was dominion. Defining dominion we see a power before us. It is a power that God gives to all His

Faith - The Working Factors

born again ones who fully accept what He says and believe it.

Jesus turns to the disciples and says, "I give you power over all the power of the enemy". Now Jesus doesn't define the enemy. The enemy in whatever form it shows itself that comes against you, is an enemy. Anything that comes to try and take you down is your enemy. Jesus just makes the statement that He has given you **power** over all the power of the enemy. It's important to see that power over you of any type that inhibits you or makes you less strong is wrong power over you and **Jesus is against it**. God is out to make sure that you get the message that you are not to suffer under any enemy *but to rise up over it.*

Look at the number of times Jesus speaks about 'the kingdom'. He says, "It is your Father's good pleasure to give you the Kingdom".

Let's look then at 'The Kingdom' for a moment. A Kingdom is where the King rules and reigns. In His land he is the supreme ruler. Nothing subverts or suppresses His wishes or desires. He is in charge of all things and the buck stops with Him.

Faith - The Working Factors

He is in charge of the Army, the Navy and the Air Force. The Police and the Security Services are all under His control. In fact the safety of the whole country is in His hands.

Jesus is our Heavenly ruler, when He rose from the dead He made the statement, "All power is given to me in Heaven and on earth". We need to see the word **'all'** and see its power value. 'All' means *'ALL'*. And then we need to see what Jesus says to the disciples in the same vein. "I give you power over **all** the power of the enemy".

The Kingdom is ours to reign in. Satan has no power here, the enemy's power that *has been* is now defeated and Jesus came to destroy all that power. The *All Power* of Jesus needs to be seen in the light that it was **He** *that created the whole universe.* Nothing was made without Him having made it. He never relinquished that power, even in death on the cross, remember Jesus said to His Father as He expired, "Father into your hands, I commend my Spirit".

Dominion is power over all things. Adam was given it immediately he was created in God's

Faith - The Working Factors

image and likeness and filled with God's breath. The new birth, being born again, is our *new* creature being created and with it comes our dominion. Look what Jesus tells the disciples to pray.... "Our Father who is in Heaven". SAY who you are, - you are a child of God, so declare it. Now call respect to His name.... ***Hallowed*** (Holy and respected) BE your name. Now call for His Kingdom to come, "Your Kingdome COME".... And "YOUR will BE done". You see, the power shift is towards you, God is telling you to take up command of the situation. This isn't a mediocre little prayer, this is chain of command being handed down from the Almighty to us.

God wants us to see more and more that we are His children and if so, then we are heirs and joint-heirs with Jesus. We share His dominion power. We dominate sin and evil, we speak in authority over them. We release liberty to captive people and loose those that are bound.

When we take up God's cause to make the world right, we get the power to do so. God empowers us by speaking His will into our faith to empower it. Our faith now becomes the spoken dominion of

Faith - The Working Factors

God that moves the mountains, whatever mountains they are. Jesus' message in Mark 11 is that if you have faith in God, you will move the mountain that is in your way and cast it into the sea, *in other words to put it out of sight*. Dominion is rule over the kingdom of darkness, dominion is your faith demanding its rights and you putting your new God given character into action. SPEAK and say to the mountain, "Be removed, get out of my sight!" It WILL obey you. Jesus said it would.

We need to see the actual, real dominion that faith has, Look in Hebrews 11 v 1…. Now faith IS. Look at the power in that statement… NOW faith is. It is power to create NOW. It's real NOW, its instant, it's NOW. Faith IS… It's here in you if you're born again, you have it. **Now** faith **is** the SUBSTANCE of things hoped for. We did the hoping, now we HAVE by faith what we hoped for. The scripture is very positive in its expression. It **IS** the EVIDENCE of things we couldn't see. If you **see** the item you prayed for, you see **faith** before you, because faith **IS** the *substance, the evidence*. You're not hoping any more, it's here!

Faith - The Working Factors

Faith has *working* factors, it is not idle, it's *active*. Faith makes us look *to see* the activity, the evidence, the substance. Faith stretches out into the future, for what we hope**d** for, to grasp the real, tangible evidence of what God promised us and bring it **now**. He said it, so it must happen, *right? There's the clue, God said it would happen if we believed.*

We have in us the living water. Once we believed Jesus, into our innermost being was deposited living water that would flow out when we needed life in any direction. Jesus didn't say a stream of living water, He said '*rivers*'. The dominion of faith flows when we feel lack. It takes hold of the situation and dominates it as we meditate on what Jesus said, on what God said.

The courage comes as we hear with our heart what the Almighty says. Then we speak. We speak the dominating word that destroys the power of satan and fear and woe and turmoil and we suppress the works of death and destruction with our dominion power. We go public with what we believe and make a show of evil and what it does. We show up the lies and the untruths that say it can't be

Faith - The Working Factors

done. We dominate the evil spiritual world and make a highway for the life of God's Spirit of life.

When you read the catalogue of what people did by their faith in Hebrews Eleven, you see what is actually, factually possible, like Jesus says.

The reason for us to have faith in God is to dominate, to have dominion, to live the higher life. We used to have a saying in one church that I attended, "Draw a line and live above it!" So draw the line. Set your goals based on what God says you can have. Glean from Scripture all the overcoming principles that cause you to think dominion power and that it is yours as a gift from the Almighty. It came with your salvation, that moment you got born again. Like Adam, you opened your eyes and lived and had dominion. You didn't have to work for it, it came with the salvation package, new life, overcoming life, powerful life.

Chapter 28
GREATER is He that is in you – the God Factor

There is one inside you that makes your Faith *live.* *This is one of the greatest faith factors of all.* We in ourselves started with nothing, no faith (none that worked for good anyway) but salvation, the *saving factor*, is what counts in all situations. God in us, is not only the 'Hope of Glory' but is the living power that provides the full answer if we listen to what He says. It matters not that we are surrounded by enemies or that we feel down and feel like running away. Elijah, a mighty, great prophet who saw God's power at work in powerful ways, heard God's still small voice. You see, it matters not that God's voice is small and quiet, what matters is what God says and the authority behind the voice. God will not holler above the noise of the enemy and compete with the enemy's noise. His peaceful and quiet voice is far more powerful than the raging storm, it always was. In fact to put a stop to the storm on the lake when the waves were raging and filling their boat, Jesus simply spoke peace, "Peace... Be still." The storm immediately obeyed Him.

Faith - The Working Factors

God's questioning voice is what we need to listen to. "What are you doing here Elijah?" In other words, 'Why are you hiding?' As Elijah hides in a cave, on the run from Jezebel, God reminds him about who He is. God causes a fire, a storm and an earthquake to pass by Elijah on the mountain. We often need to see some demonstration of God's power to push our faith back into action but all we need to do is remember what the still small voice of God says. Greater is the one in you. Greater is the authority and Spirit that is resident in your being. Jesus said, "If you believe in me, out of your innermost being shall flow rivers of living water.

Never mind the stormy waves of water that would try and drown you; inside you are rivers of living water. This is not death water, this is *living* water, rivers of it, resident in you *waiting to flow and destroy the death motivated waters*. You have in you something that flows from heavens throne. John sees it and describes it in the book of revelation….. "Revelation 22:1 KJV

Faith - The Working Factors

"And he showed me *a pure river of water of life*, clear as crystal, proceeding *out of the throne of God and of the Lamb.*"

The rivers of life that we have in us are pure and unadulterated and flow out of God's throne of authority and out of God Himself. Because there is no malice in God, there is no weakness or *bad* behaviour in Him, only goodness, therefore He is all powerful. That river of life we have in us comes from *His* source and can therefore do anything. The 'anythings' are generated by His faith that we have. Faith IS the substance of what we hope for, the evidence of it. It is what we *see* happen in the event when faith *brings* a miracle.
GREATER is He that is in you.... Focus on Him that saved you from sin and death, He is resident in you when you are born again.

You know, many have doubts arise when they begin to use their faith and satan often says, as does our own flesh sometimes, "Aaah you're not born again, you're the same old so and so that you always were." Well there's a very simple way to fix that, just stand before God and say, "Father God in Heaven, I come to you and ask for

Faith - The Working Factors

forgiveness and ask you to cleanse me from all my sin and come live in me by your Spirit and make me a new creature as you promised and be my sovereign Lord!" Now turn to satan and say clearly, "Don't you ever question my salvation or whether I'm born again, ever!"

You see, there is always an answer to every problem when you take up your faith factors and use them.

We are not the losers or the ones with no answer. With God we always have an answer. God has invested in us His nature, His overcoming words and therefore His power to do what needs to be done.

Life must be the order of the day. Death and all the weak stuff must be put to flight, it's what Jesus *said* we should have, 'I give you power over all the power of the enemy'. So learn to speak faith. If you have never spoken faith, then make a start. Start speaking to the problems, faith needs to be spoken out and go public for it to happen. This is where the authority lies, in speaking it out and demanding it to be so.

Faith - The Working Factors

It's sometimes difficult to grasp that we have in us the Almighty God, resident by His Spirit in us but this is who we are now. Just accept it. Say, 'Thank you Father, I accept you in all your power and authority, remove all the weaknesses and doubts, live fully in me'. AMEN (so be it).

The 'so be it' is so important. We always have the last word over satan. However much he tries to argue his way out of things and try and discuss terms, *we have the last word.* **God always gives you the last word.**

The great factor of faith is that you have dominion over all things when you need it. The world started that way with Adam and it is restored in us through salvation when we are born again.

God bless your faith as you read His words and hear His teaching and bring alive in you His will and purpose. God motivate His faith inside you and give you great Peace and overcoming Love and Joy! **The Lord be with you.**

'Taste and SEE that the Lord is good'.

Faith will provide the proof of His good nature His goodness.

Printed in Great Britain
by Amazon